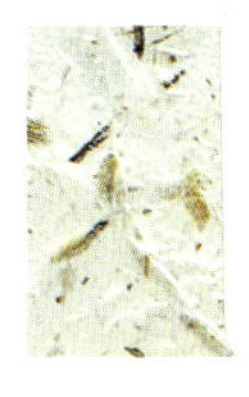

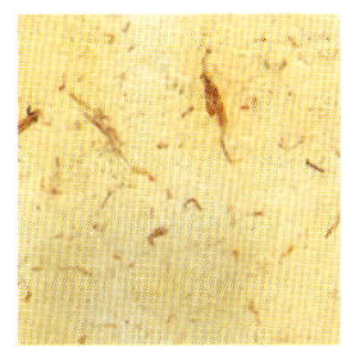

papermaking techniques book

papermaking techniques book

Over 50 techniques for making and embellishing handmade paper

John Plowman

contents

A QUANTUM BOOK

This book was produced by
Quantum Books Ltd
6 Blundell Street
London N7 9BH

This edition printed 2010

ISBN: 978-1-84573-244-8

QUMPATE

Printed in Singapore by
Star Standard Industries
(Pte) Ltd

Using color

Dry papers

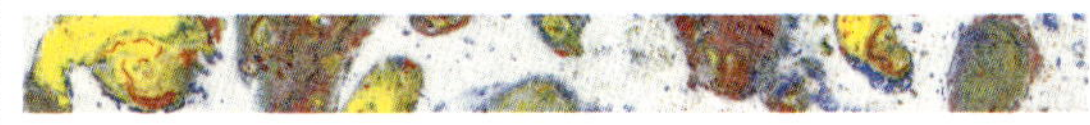

Introduction

PAPER is an integral part of our lives today, from the newspaper we read to the packaging we nonchalantly throw away every day. We don't give it a second thought, assuming that paper, like everything else, must be the end product of a very sophisticated process. Nothing could be further from the truth. Unbelievable as it may seem, the basic principle of making paper today is exactly the same as when it was first discovered in China 2,000 years ago.

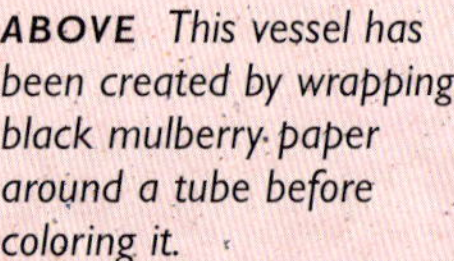

ABOVE *This vessel has been created by wrapping black mulberry paper around a tube before coloring it.*

A sheet of paper, whether made by hand or in a large paper mill, is a mass of interlocking fibers held together by cellulose. Cellulose is a naturally occurring substance found in plant fibers. A sheet of paper is formed by suspending these fibers in water and immersing a mold (a rectangular frame with mesh stretched across) with a deckle (a same size rectangular frame) on top,

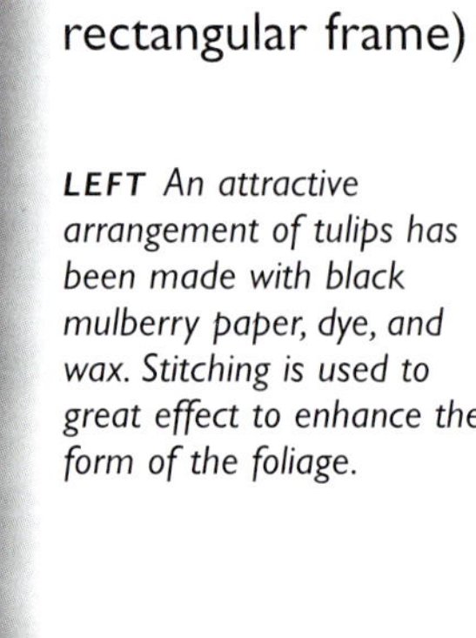

LEFT *An attractive arrangement of tulips has been made with black mulberry paper, dye, and wax. Stitching is used to great effect to enhance the form of the foliage.*

RIGHT *The versatility of paper is explored in this sculpture where pulp made from recycled white envelopes has been poured onto thorn branches fixed to a frame, thereby embedding them in the large sheet of paper.*

into the water. As the mold and deckle are lifted out, a layer of interlocking fibers is left on the surface of the mold, the deckle's purpose being to keep these fibers in place. The water enables the cellulose in the fibers to expand, so aiding their bonding together. Although most of the water drains away as the mold and deckle are lifted out, some still remains in the

BELOW *Paper made with cotton linters pulp was laminated. After sizing, the final finish was achieved by scratching into a wax resist and painting with thin washes of acrylic paint.*

sheet, which needs to be carefully removed from the mold before the final pressing and drying process.

A readily available source of suitable fibers is an essential requirement for papermaking. The most economic and easily found source is paper, which can be recycled to make new sheets. Part-processed fibers are available, in sheet form, from a specialist supplier (see page 124), while using a plant material as your source of fiber means you will be starting completely from scratch. When using any plant material the first task is to cook it in an alkaline solution; this facilitates the breaking down of the fibers, enabling them to absorb water, and removes any

BELOW *Entitled "Beneath the Surface," this piece comprises five sections, each made with cotton linters pulp and ready-made paper inclusions.*

LEFT
A web structure made with cotton linters pulp, into which the artist has combined embroidery and a linocut printed on waxed cartridge paper.

RIGHT *Paper rolls were manipulated by hand to create a bowl shape, which was then cut into with an electric saw to create the dramatic fringe effect.*

LEFT *Paper made from recycled newspaper and packaging has been painted, stitched, and inlaid with silk and pearls to create a colorful hanging.*

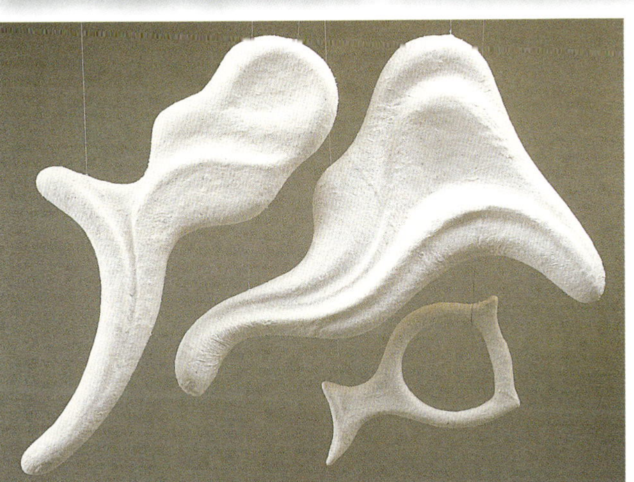

LEFT *Entitled "Listen III," these three hanging forms were made by casting acid-free cotton recycled pulp around clay models.*

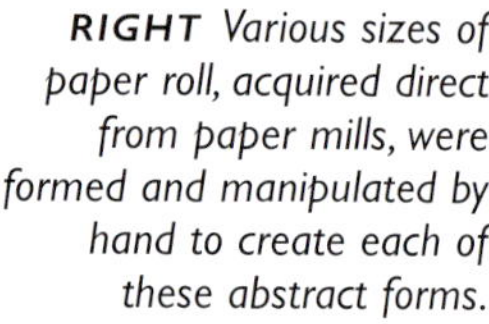

RIGHT *Various sizes of paper roll, acquired direct from paper mills, were formed and manipulated by hand to create each of these abstract forms.*

impurities. The cooking process is complete when the plant material produces a neutral pH reading. Whatever the source of fiber, it needs to be beaten to separate its constituent fibers. Initially this would have been done by hand, but over the centuries this process has evolved and is now mechanized. For the purposes of this book an everyday food blender will suffice.

In the pages that follow I intend to show you how straightforward it is to make your own paper— and I can assure you that there is nothing difficult about it. When following these techniques think positively, and if at first you don't succeed, try again. Believe me, it won't be long before you are proficient enough at these techniques to have a go at the five projects also included. After that, the world is your oyster, and I hope that, like me, you find papermaking an enjoyable and creative experience.

ABOVE *"Sharp Tongues–Soft Knives" is the title of this two-piece work. Paper made from cotton linters pulp has been laminated, painted, and waxed.*

RIGHT *This bowl is made with black mulberry paper. The rim is made with corrugated paper and embellished with stitching and beads.*

LEFT *Sheets of paper made with pulp colored with fabric dye were further colored with metallic paint, then torn into strips and machine-stitched together to create this interlocking composition.*

BELOW *Paper rolls were used to create a layered effect, and then carefully manipulated and built up by hand to create this paper vessel.*

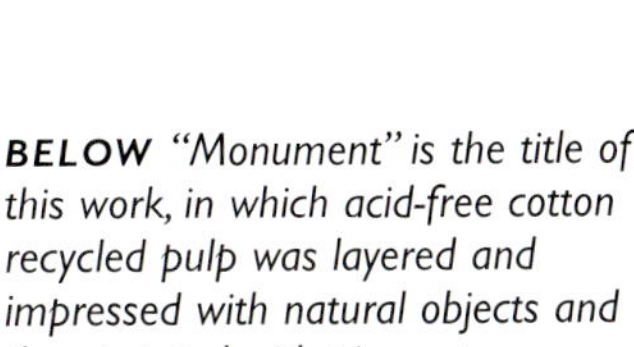

BELOW *"Monument" is the title of this work, in which acid-free cotton recycled pulp was layered and impressed with natural objects and then painted with pigments.*

Before you start

You will find that some of the equipment you need to make paper is relatively close to hand, such as a food blender, a plastic tub, or disposable cleaning cloths that are readily available in the supermarket. Other items of equipment can be made quite easily with the minimum of effort.

In the following step-by-step techniques, you will learn how to make the basic pieces of equipment needed to embark on the

***ABOVE** The equipment you need to create your own paper can be easily found or made at home.*

Making a mold and deckle

YOU WILL NEED

- **4 6 in (15cm) lengths of 1 x ¾ in (2.5 x 2cm) soft wood**
- **4 10 in (25cm) lengths of 1 x ¾ in (2.5 x 2cm) soft wood**
- **Waterproof wood glue**
- **Adjustable corner clamp**
- **Electric drill**
- **⅛ in (0.3cm) drill bit**
- **Countersink**
- **1½ in (4cm) non-corrosive screws**
- **Screwdriver**
- **Acrylic varnish**
- **Paintbrush**
- **Scissors**
- **Fine-gauge aluminum mesh**
- **Staple gun and staples**
- **Waterproof tape**
- **Craft knife**

1 Apply waterproof wood glue to the end of a 6 in (15cm) length of soft wood. Position this at right angles to a 10 in (25cm) length in a corner clamp. Drill a pilot hole into both pieces, countersink the hole, and screw the two pieces together. Repeat until each of the four sides of the frame are screwed together. Make a second frame in the same way.

2 Apply a coat of acrylic varnish to waterproof the frames. Leave to dry.

3 Cut a 7 x 9 in (18 x 23cm) piece of fine-gauge aluminum mesh. This is slightly smaller than the outside dimensions of the frame.

4 Position the mesh centrally on top of one of the frames. Hold a staple gun over the mesh in the center of one side and staple the mesh to the frame. Move to the opposite side, pull the mesh taut across the frame, and staple. Repeat on the remaining two sides. Staple all along the edges to secure the mesh to the frame.

5 Cover the jagged edge of the mesh with waterproof tape, taking

adventure of making your first sheet of paper. The most important is the mold and deckle, basically two frames of the same size, either rectangular or shaped, one with a fine mesh stretched over it, called the mold, the other, which fits directly on top, called the deckle. These items can be bought specifically for papermaking, individually or as part of a papermaking kit, or, as shown here, you can simply adapt picture frames or embroidery hoops. The other essential piece of equipment is a press, used to force water from the formed sheets of paper. This is is easily made from fiberboard and a few bolts.

***ABOVE** Two wooden picture frames of the same size can be adapted to make a deckle.*

care not to tape over the inside edge of the frame. If the tape is wider than the frame the excess can be trimmed off with a craft knife.

6 The mold is now complete and the deckle, the other frame, fits on top. Always hold the mold with the taped edges uppermost and the deckle tightly on top. The same method can be used to make any size of mold and deckle, such as the second mold and deckle pictured here that is double the size of the first.

Using picture frames

YOU WILL NEED

- **2 8 x 6 in (20 x 15cm) picture frames**
- **Acrylic varnish**
- **Paintbrush**
- **Net curtain fabric**
- **Scissors**
- **Staple gun and staples**
- **Waterproof tape**
- **Craft knife**

1 Waterproof both picture frames by applying a coat of acrylic varnish. Leave to dry.

2 Cut a piece of net curtain fabric larger than the picture frame. Staple the net to the center of one side of the frame, and all along the edge at 1 in (2.5cm) intervals. Move to the opposite side and pull the net taut across the frame, and staple as before. Repeat on the remaining two sides.

3 Trim away excess fabric around the frame midway between the outside edges and the staples.

4 Stick waterproof tape over the staples and trim flush to the edge of the frame with a craft knife.

5 The other picture frame is used as the deckle and fits snugly on top. Hold the mold with the taped edges uppermost and the deckle tightly on top.

Whatever your choice of mesh for stretching across the mold, check that the size of the holes does not exceed 1⁄16 in (2mm) square. This ensures that the sheet you form contains fibers that are closely matted together. If the holes are any bigger, the fibers will fall through them as the mold is lifted out of the vat. When this happens, it results in a weaker sheet of loosely matted fibers. Of course, you can use an even finer mesh, such as net

LEFT A piece of mesh and a few lengths of wood are the basic ingredients for making a shaped mold and deckle.

Making a shaped mold and deckle

YOU WILL NEED

- **2 12 in (30cm) lengths of 1 x ¾ in (2.5 x 2cm) soft wood**
- **2 9 in (23cm) lengths of 1 x ¾ in (2.5 x 2cm) soft wood**
- **2 6¾ in (17cm) lengths of 1 x ¾ in (2.5 x 2cm) soft wood**
- **Miter saw**
- **Waterproof wood glue**
- **Adjustable corner clamp**
- **Electric drill**
- **⅛ in (0.3cm) drill bit**
- **Countersink**
- **1½ in (4cm) non-corrosive screws**
- **Screwdriver**
- **Acrylic varnish**
- **Paintbrush**
- **Scissors**
- **Fine-gauge aluminum mesh**
- **Staple gun and staples**
- **Waterproof tape**
- **Craft knife**

1 Use a miter saw to cut 45° and 90° angles on three different lengths of soft wood. Cut a 45° angle at each end of the two longest pieces, so that their longest sides still measure 12 in (30cm). Cut a 90° and 45° angle at either end of the mid-length and shortest pieces, so that their longest sides still measure 9 in (23cm) and 6¾ in (17cm).

2 Apply waterproof wood glue to the end of a short piece of wood. Position this at right angles to a mid-length piece in a corner clamp. Drill a pilot hole into both pieces, countersink the hole, and screw the two pieces together.

3 Adjust the corner clamp to its 45° setting. Apply glue to the angled ends of the longest piece and place in the clamp so that its outside edge lines up with the angle on the end of each of the other two pieces. Drill, countersink, and screw the three pieces together. Make a second frame in the same way.

4 Apply a coat of acrylic varnish to waterproof the frames. Leave to dry.

5 Cut a piece of fine-gauge aluminum mesh slightly smaller than the outside dimensions of the frame. Follow steps 4–5 of Making a Mold and Deckle (see page 12) to complete the mold.

6 The other shaped frame fits over the top of the mold as the deckle. Hold the mold with the taped edges uppermost and the deckle tightly on top.

RIGHT For a ready-made shaped mold and deckle, embroidery hoops are ideal.

curtain fabric, but remember the closer the weave the longer it will take for the water to drain away.

There are other alternatives to net curtain fabric, such as the fine mesh used in gardening, or dressmaking net fabric, but always test the material's strength because it can tear very easily when stretched across the mold.

Using embroidery hoops

YOU WILL NEED

- **Embroidery hoops**
- **Acrylic varnish**
- **Paintbrush**
- **Net curtain fabric**
- **Scissors**

1 Separate the inner and outer embroidery hoops and then coat each hoop with a coat of acrylic varnish in order to ensure that they are waterproof.

3 Trim away the excess net as close as possible to the edge of the hoops.

2 Lay the outer hoop on a flat surface. Place a piece of net curtain fabric over the hoop and press the inner hoop firmly in place. If the outer hoop has a tightening screw, use this to further secure the net.

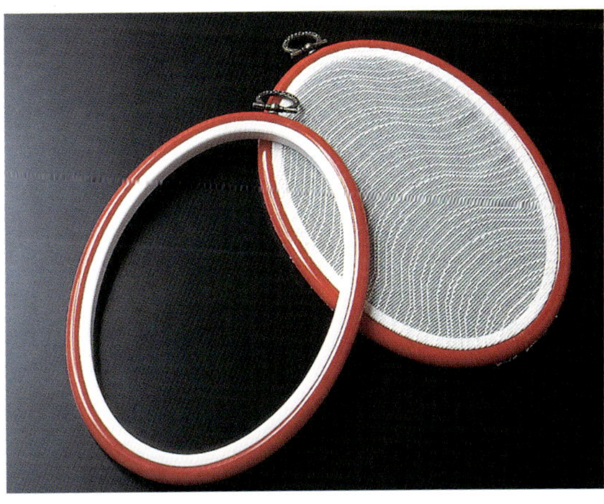

4 Embroidery hoops quickly and easily make a very serviceable mold and deckle with the minimum of fuss.

***RIGHT** Attractively shaped papers can be used for party invitations or place names at a dinner table.*

Foamboard is an economic material that is easy to cut into, and you will come across its use in other parts of the book. When using foamboard it is essential that you paint on two coats of acrylic varnish to provide a waterproof coating and so extend its life. Although foamboard's main drawback is its short life expectancy, if used with care and attention it should work well and last long enough for you to master the basics of forming a shaped sheet of paper.

Making a shaped deckle only

YOU WILL NEED

- **Mold and deckle (see pages 12–13)**
- **⅛ in (0.3cm) thick foamboard**
- **Pencil**
- **Shaped object**
- **Cutting mat**
- **Craft knife**
- **Acrylic varnish**
- **Paintbrush**

1 Place your wooden deckle on the foamboard, aligning it along the two edges of the board. Draw around the other two sides of the deckle.

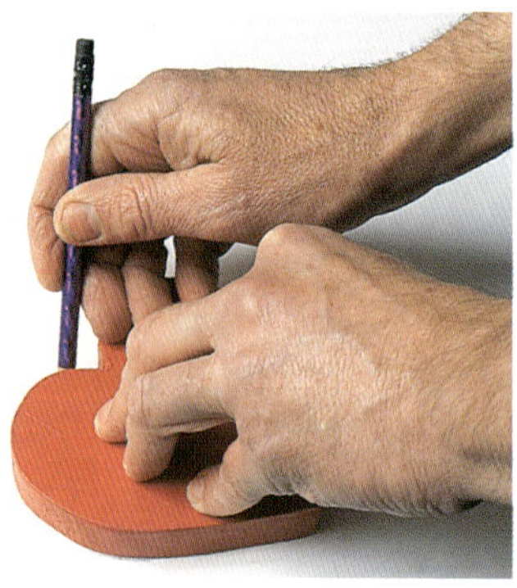

2 Place a shaped object centrally within the deckle outline on the foamboard and draw around it.

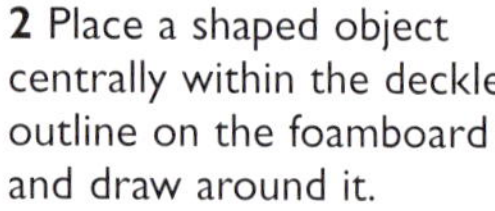

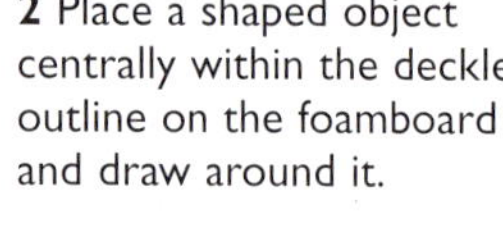

3 On a cutting mat, use a craft knife to carefully cut along the pencil line, aiming to keep to one clean, unbroken cut.

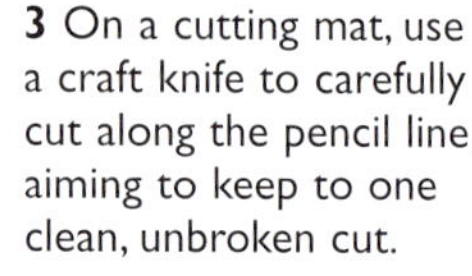

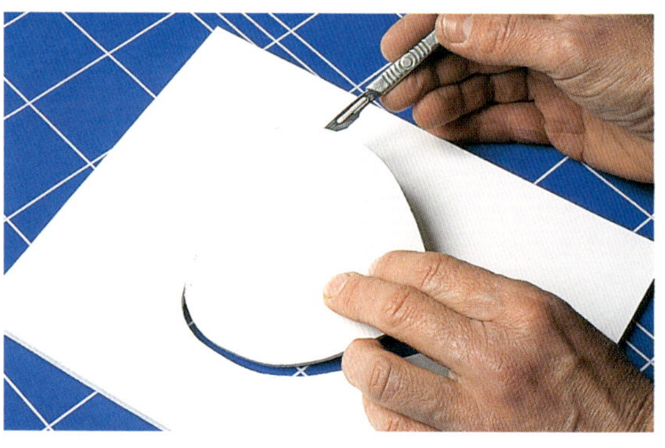

4 To increase the life span of the foamboard give the shape a coat of acrylic varnish. The shaped deckle is used with the usual mold (see Sheet Forming with a Shaped Deckle, page 35).

***LEFT** Any simple outline can be used when you make a shaped deckle. Choose a shape that is not too intricate.*

***RIGHT** All types of paper are pressed in the same way. From left to right: paper made from recycled pulp, plant pulp, cotton linters pulp, and kraft pulp.*

The press is an essential piece of equipment but it is not absolutely necessary that you make a press yourself. Instead you could use two sheets of fiberboard between which you can sandwich the wet formed sheets and use either weights or clamps to apply the required pressure to expel the excess water.

Making a press

YOU WILL NEED

- **2 10 x 12 x ½ in (25 x 30 x 1.5cm) pieces of fiberboard**
- **Straightedge**
- **Pencil**
- **Tape measure**
- **G-clamps**
- **Electric drill**
- **⅜ in (1cm) drill bit**
- **Acrylic varnish**
- **Paintbrush**
- **4 3 in (7.5cm) long and ¼ in (0.6mm) diameter bolts**
- **4 wing nuts**

1 On one of the 10 x 12 x ½ in (25 x 30 x 1.5cm) pieces of fiberboard, use a straightedge to draw two diagonal lines from corner to corner. Measure and mark 1½ in (4cm) in from each corner on the line.

2 With the sheet you have marked on top, clamp the two fiberboard pieces together, making sure their edges are flush all the way around.

3 Hold an electric drill vertically and place the drill bit on one of the marks. Carefully drill down through both sheets of fiberboard. Repeat the drilling on the remaining three marks.

4 Unclamp the sheets and apply acrylic varnish to all surfaces, painting one side at a time, leaving each to dry before continuing. Don't forget the edges.

5 Place a bolt in each hole of one sheet only, then lower the other sheet over the top to fit onto the bolts.

6 Screw on the wing nuts to make a serviceable press. It is easy to make a larger press, for instance the second press pictured complements the larger mold and deckle made earlier (see page 13). The dimensions are doubled but the size of the holes and bolts remains the same.

making paper

The following pages take you through the essentials of papermaking, from preparing pulp and sheet forming, to pressing and drying. Once you have become proficient at making a sheet of paper it is just a small step to tackle new techniques and further develop your papermaking skills.

Making pulp from recycled paper

Pulp is the fiber source with which a sheet of paper is made. There are three techniques for preparing pulps from three different fiber sources. The first uses recycled paper, a readily available source, so start saving the everyday household paper that you would normally throw away. Although newspaper seems to be the most obvious source of wastepaper, be aware that it tends to make a weak sheet, so

ABOVE *In this piece, entitled "Minutiae," the artist has used watercolor on hand-cast paper.*

YOU WILL NEED

- **Wastepaper**
- **Scissors**
- **Saucepan, used solely for papermaking**
- **Wooden spoon, used solely for papermaking**
- **Strainer**
- **2 pint (1.2l) food blender**
- **Net curtain fabric**

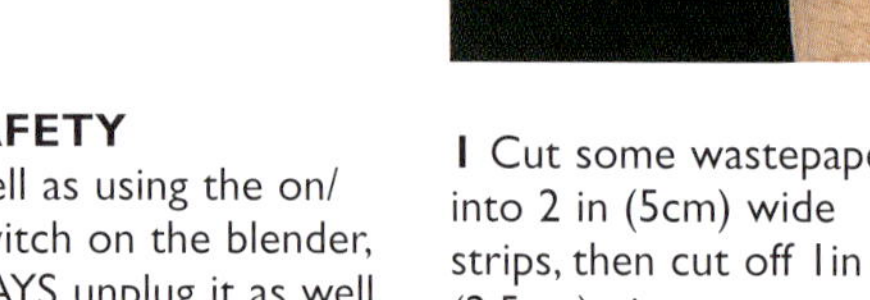

SAFETY
As well as using the on/off switch on the blender, ALWAYS unplug it as well.

1 Cut some wastepaper into 2 in (5cm) wide strips, then cut off 1in (2.5cm) pieces.

2 Half fill a saucepan with water and bring to the boil. Carefully add the paper scraps and use a wooden spoon to completely immerse them. Don't put so many scraps in that they cannot all be covered with water. Turn down the heat and let the water simmer for 30 minutes. This will rid the paper of some of its ink and other impurities.

3 Empty the contents of the pan into a strainer and thoroughly rinse in cold water.

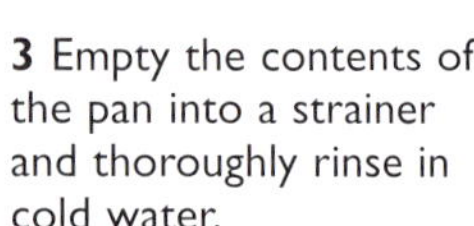

RIGHT *Constructed paper made from recycled pulp has been placed on a silver background with threads.*

choose circulars, letters, envelopes, or packaging instead. If you can get it, another good source of recyclable paper is shredded office waste.

RIGHT *Metallic threads, tissue paper, fabric dyes, and metallic and acrylic paints have been used on recycled pulp paper.*

4 Half fill a 2 pint (1.2l) food blender jug with water and add two small handfuls of boiled paper.

5 Operate the blender In short, 30-second bursts until the paper has been completely broken down. If the blender labors too much, switch it off (unplug it as well) and take out some of the pulp, add more water, and start again.

6 Empty the pulp into a strainer lined with net curtain fabric and let the water drain out.

7 Squeeze the remaining water from the pulp and store it in an airtight plastic container until you are ready to use it.

Making pulp from part-processed fibers

You can obtain part-processed fibers from a specialist papermaking supplier (see Suppliers, page 124). It comes in sheet form and, as the name suggests, a lot of the preparation work has already been done. Cotton linters are most commonly used, and bought in sheets. With these fibers you can always be certain of creating a sheet of paper that is consistent in color and texture, especially good for writing, drawing, or painting on.

YOU WILL NEED

- **Sheet of cotton linters**
- **Bowl**
- **2 pint (1.2l) food blender**
- **Strainer**
- **Net curtain fabric**

1 Tear off roughly 1 in (2.5cm) squares from a sheet of cotton linters, and leave to soak overnight in a bowl of water. This will loosen up the fibers in the sheet and make them easier to beat in the blender.

Tearing the cotton linters into small pieces will make it easier to beat the fibers in a blender after they have been soaked overnight.

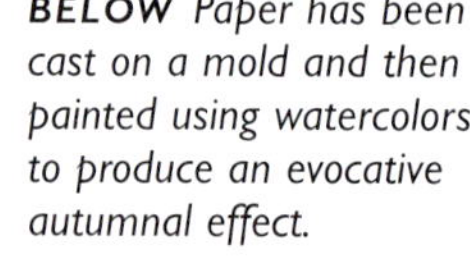

BELOW *Paper has been cast on a mold and then painted using watercolors to produce an evocative autumnal effect.*

2 Place two small handfuls of the soaked strips into a 2 pint (1.2l) blender jug and fill with water to the halfway mark.

LEFT *The artist used cotton linters pulp to make this delicate paper that is embedded with threads, petals, and fibers.*

Squeezing every last drop of water out of the pulp ensures that it dries quickly if you intend to save it for later use. See page 27 for storage suggestions.

3 Operate the blender in short, 30-second bursts until the paper has been completely broken down. If the cotton linter strips were well soaked they should only need about three minutes beating time. Do not overfill the blender and do not labor the motor. As soon as it starts to give off strange noises switch it off (unplug it as well), remove some pulp, add more water, and start again.

4 Pour the pulp into a strainer lined with net curtain fabric. To get the remaining water out of the pulp form a bag around the pulp and pull the net fabric back up through your thumb and forefinger.

5 Other types of part-processed fibers can be prepared in the same way. In the picture above, the white pulp is the cotton linters. Esparta—the off-white pulp—is weaker than cotton and produces a textured sheet. The brown pulp, called kraft, makes strong paper. Formed kraft sheets are used to make covers and boxes.

Making pulp from plant fibers

The final technique for making pulp uses plant material as the fiber source, and it is this method that lets you really experiment with what you can find in your own locality. Fibrous plants make good paper: carefully tear along the length of a plant stem, splitting it lengthwise as far as you can, to get some idea of its fibrous potential.

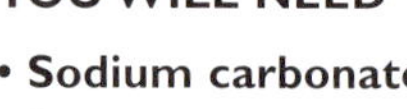

YOU WILL NEED

- **Sodium carbonate**
- **Saucepan, not aluminum, used solely for papermaking**
- **pH test strips**
- **Plant material**
- **Scissors**
- **Wooden spoon, used solely for papermaking**
- **Strainer**
- **Net curtain fabric**
- **2 pint (1.2l) food blender**
- **Chopping board**
- **Wooden mallet**
- **Glass container**
- **Airtight plastic containers or freezer bags**

1 To make an alkaline solution, add 8 oz (225g) of sodium carbonate to 2 pints (1.2l) of water in a saucepan.

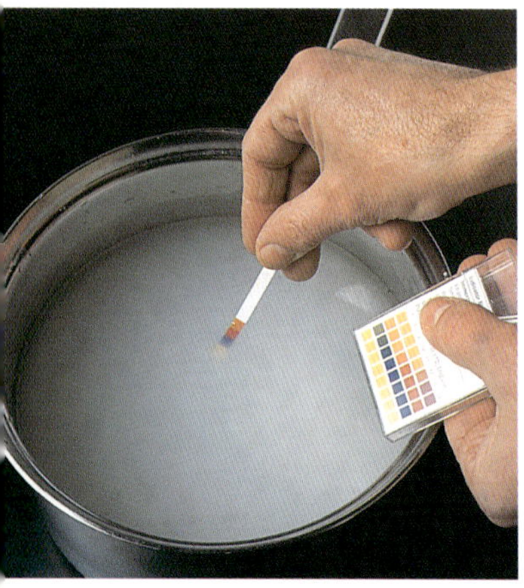

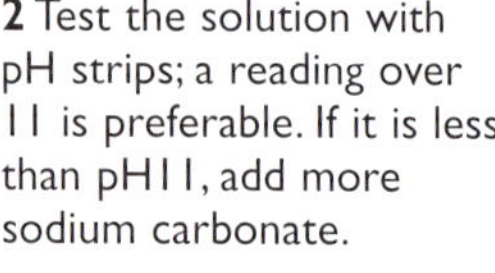

2 Test the solution with pH strips; a reading over 11 is preferable. If it is less than pH11, add more sodium carbonate.

3 Cut your plant material into manageable lengths and add to the alkaline solution, using a wooden spoon to fully immerse the pieces. It is important that they are all submersed.

4 Bring the alkaline solution and plant material to the boil, then turn down the heat and simmer for 3 hours. The impurities that have been removed from the plant material will turn the solution a murky brown color. Leave to cool.

LEFT AND FAR LEFT
The artist who produced these pieces experiments with a variety of plant fibers to achieve different colors, including bearded iris, onion skin, and bracken.

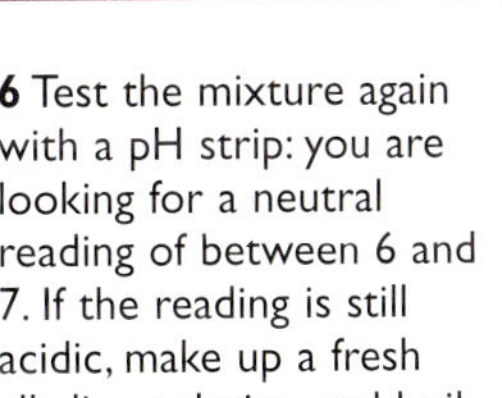

6 Test the mixture again with a pH strip: you are looking for a neutral reading of between 6 and 7. If the reading is still acidic, make up a fresh alkaline solution and boil the same plant material again. As you experiment with different types of plant material you will become more versed in the amount of time each needs to be boiled.

5 Empty the saucepan into a strainer lined with net curtain fabric and thoroughly rinse in cold water until the water runs clear out of the strainer.

7 The plant material will have become quite matted after boiling, so spend some time separating it.

RIGHT This stunning effect is achieved by the artist pouring pulp onto leaves and leaf skeletons, then finishing with painting and stitching.

Long, strong grasses are great, so for this example I have used wild plants and flowers that grow around the fields where I live. Plant stems are also a good source of fibers, so why not find a friendly florist who will let you have any unsold stems before they are discarded. You could also try vegetables such as leeks or celery, or even come up with something completely new.

Because of the seasonal availability of plant fiber it is advisable to produce a good-sized batch of pulp in one session. You can also dry beaten plant fiber for long-term storage.

8 Half fill a 2 pint (1.2l) blender jug with water and add a handful of plant material.

9 Operate the blender in short bursts to beat and separate the fibers. The plant material will wrap itself around the blades of the blender, so switch it off and unplug it, then untangle the material.

10 It is preferable to mix long and short fibers to make a strong sheet of paper. Fibers produced in the blender are short. To get longer fibers, spread a handful of the material on a chopping board and pound with a mallet until separated into long lengths.

11 You can test the length of the fibers by adding some to a glass of water and stirring them around. The glass on the left, above, contains short fibers beaten in a blender, while the longer fibers on the right were beaten with a mallet.

RIGHT *Handmade paper was layered and impressed with stones, before being painted with pigments.*

12 Mix the short and long fibers together. I suggest a ratio of 2 parts short fibers to 1 part long, but it is really up to you to decide—there are no hard and fast rules.

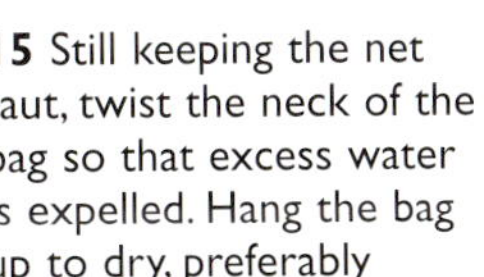

13 If you intend to use the prepared plant fiber in the next week, it can be adequately stored in airtight plastic containers or in freezer bags with airtight seals.

14 To store plant pulp for much later use, return the material to the net curtain fabric. Form the net into a bag and pull it up through your thumb and forefinger to squeeze out the water.

15 Still keeping the net taut, twist the neck of the bag so that excess water is expelled. Hang the bag up to dry, preferably outside on a bright windy day, or over a radiator. Once dry, remove from the net and store in an airtight container.

16 When it is time to use the fiber, simply reconstitute by carefully separating the dried fibers and rehydrating them by soaking overnight in a bowl of water.

Sheet forming

As there is a lot of water involved in making paper, the closer you are to a water supply and sink the easier it will be for you. Also make sure your work surface and floor are adequately protected from spills and splashes.

You have prepared the equipment and raw materials and are now ready to make your first sheet of paper. The process, from beginning to end, consists of four

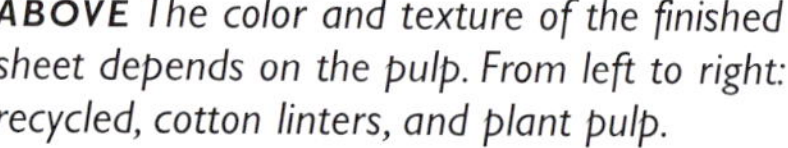

ABOVE *The color and texture of the finished sheet depends on the pulp. From left to right: recycled, cotton linters, and plant pulp.*

Sheet forming with recycled paper pulp

YOU WILL NEED

- **Recycled paper pulp (see pages 20–21)**
- **Vat, any large plastic container**
- **Wooden implement for stirring**
- **Mold and deckle (see pages 12–13)**

1 Half fill the vat with warm water and add the recycled paper pulp. Aim for a consistency similar to that of pancake batter. As a general rule the more pulp you put in, the thicker your sheet of paper will be. With practice you will be able to gauge the correct quantity.

2 Stir the pulp well so that it is evenly distributed around the water in the vat, ensuring that there are no lumps.

3 Immediately after stirring the pulp mixture to a smooth consistency, position the deckle on top of the mold and hold both vertically over the vat at arm's length.

LEFT *This sheet was formed from small layers, some stenciled to provide the patttern. Gold leaf was scattered on the surface while forming the sheet.*

separate operations: sheet forming, couching, pressing, and drying.

Forming a sheet of paper with the mold and deckle is the same process regardless of the type of fiber pulp you use. However, if you wish to write, draw, or paint on the paper you make it is advisable to size it beforehand. Size can be bought from art and craft suppliers. It can be added to the pulp in the vat so that the sheet you make is more resistant to inks

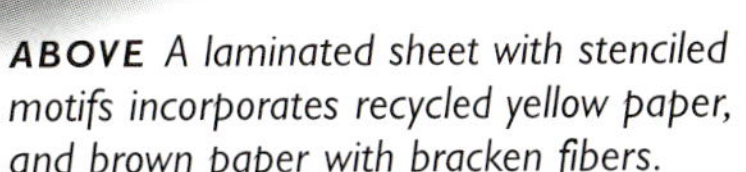

ABOVE *A laminated sheet with stenciled motifs incorporates recycled yellow paper, and brown paper with bracken fibers.*

4 Hold the mold and deckle firmly and steadily, and in one continuous movement, maneuver them vertically into the vat. As they enter the pulp mixture bring them into a horizontal position.

6 Holding the mold and deckle tightly together, tip them at a slight diagonal to let the last drops of water drain off.

5 Bring the mold and deckle horizontally up through the water, gently shaking them from side to side to evenly distribute the pulp across the mold. Remain in this position to allow the water to drain off the mold.

7 Hold the mold horizontally in one hand and lift off the deckle, taking care not to let any water drip onto the formed sheet of paper.

and paints, reducing the likelihood of color bleeding. I use a commercial brand of size, but you could also use gelatin, wallpaper size, or craft glue (PVA). Adding size to the vat is illustrated in the Sheet Forming with Part-processed Fiber Pulp technique below, but you can add it, in the same way, to any type of pulp. Recycled paper pulp made from printed matter does not need sizing, because the paper would already have been sized in the first instance.

LEFT This dramatic piece, entitled "Ceremonial," is 59 in (150cm) long. The artist used cotton linters pulp and laminated directly onto the wet sheet.

RIGHT Cotton linters pulp was used to create "Blue Opening," a triptych that has been laminated, painted, and waxed.

8 If you do happen to drip water onto the formed sheet, or touch the sheet with the deckle when removing it, as illustrated here, the sheet can be easily removed from the mold.

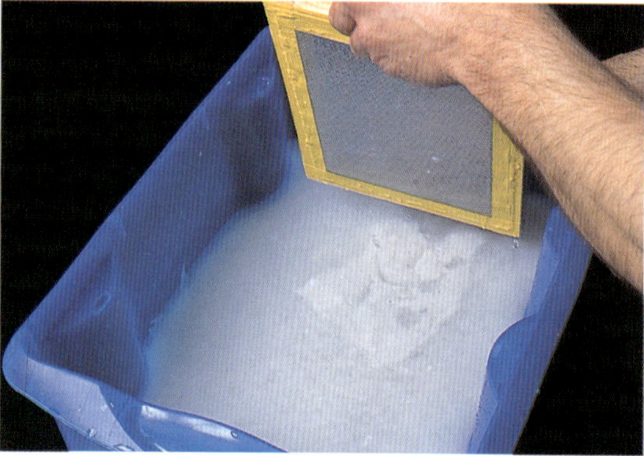

9 Turn the mold over, parallel to the surface of the water. Let the formed sheet touch the surface and quickly lift up the mold. The damaged sheet will be left in the vat. Stir the sheet back into the pulp and start sheet forming again.

Sheet forming with part-processed fiber pulp

YOU WILL NEED

- **Vat, any large plastic container**
- **Measuring jug**
- **Size**
- **Cotton linters pulp (see pages 22–23)**
- **Wooden implement for stirring**
- **Mold and deckle (see pages 12–13)**

1 Half fill the vat with warm water. Make up a solution of size according to the manufacturer's instructions and then add it to the vat.

2 Add the cotton linters pulp. As a general rule the more you put in, the thicker your sheet of paper will be. As a guideline, aim for the consistency of pancake batter. With experience you will be able to judge the amount of pulp required for different thicknesses of paper.

3 Stir the pulp well so that it is evenly distributed around the water in the vat and lump free.

4 Follow steps 3–7 of Sheet Forming with Recycled Paper Pulp (see page 28), and steps 8–9 if necessary.

LEFT *Recycled paper pulp is formed into shapes without a mold and deckle.*

When you add any type of pulp to the vat prior to sheet forming, it is essential that it is stirred and left to sit for 15 minutes before being stirred again. This process will ensure that the fibers have separated and float freely in the vat. If you do not do this your formed sheet of paper may have lumps of pulp embedded in the surface. If this is the case, return the sheet to the vat and stir and leave for a while longer to allow the fibers to separate.

LEFT *The artist made this triptych from cotton linters pulp, then cut out two squares, which were cut up and stitched. The squares were then stitched in place before painting and waxing.*

Sheet forming with plant fiber pulp

YOU WILL NEED

- **Plant fiber pulp (see pages 24–25)**
- **Vat, any large plastic container**
- **Mold and deckle (see pages 12–13)**

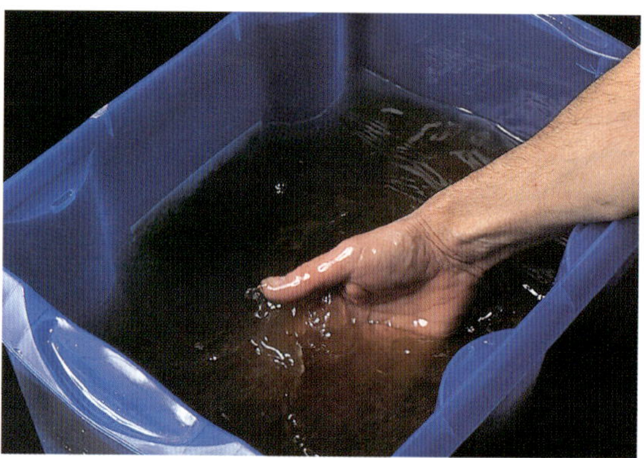

2 Thoroughly mix the plant fibers into the water so that they are evenly distributed around the vat.

1 Half fill the vat with warm water. Before you add the pulp, separate the fibers by hand. I have used three handfuls in this half-full vat which measures 16 x 12 in (41 x 30cm), and is 10 in (25cm) high. The vat must be big enough for you to maneuver your mold and deckle.

3 Follow steps 3–7 of Sheet Forming with Recycled Paper Pulp (see pages 28–29), and steps 8–9 if necessary.

It is also worth experimenting with mixing different types of pulp together to form a sheet. I suggest a 50:50 mix of plant fiber and cotton linters pulp.

LEFT *A shaped deckle can be used with all types of pulp. Shown here from left to right is kraft, esparta, and recycled pulp papers.*

Sheet forming with a shaped mold and deckle

YOU WILL NEED

- **Pulp in the vat (see pages 28–29)**
- **Shaped mold and deckle (see page 14)**

2 In one continuous movement, maneuver the mold and deckle vertically into the vat, and as they enter the pulp mixture bring them into a horizontal position.

1 Don't worry if you find this process a bit more awkward. Immediately after stirring the vat of pulp, hold the shaped mold and deckle tightly together vertically over the vat.

3 Bring the mold and deckle horizontally up through the water, gently shaking them from side to side to evenly distribute the pulp across the mold. Remain in this position to allow the water to drain off the mold.

▶

RIGHT Paper made with plant fiber pulp has a characteristic texture caused by the length of the fibers.

LEFT The stunning 3-D effect of this piece was achieved by layering sheets made with various shapes of frame.

4 Still holding the mold and deckle tightly together, tip them at a slight angle to let the last drops of water drain off.

5 Hold the mold horizontally in one hand and lift off the deckle, taking care not to let any water drip onto the formed sheet of paper. If you do drip water onto the formed sheet, or touch the sheet with the deckle when removing it, follow step 9 of Sheet Forming with Recycled Paper Pulp (see page 30).

Sheet forming with embroidery hoops

YOU WILL NEED

- **Pulp in the vat (see pages 28–29)**
- **Embroidery hoop mold and deckle (see page 15)**

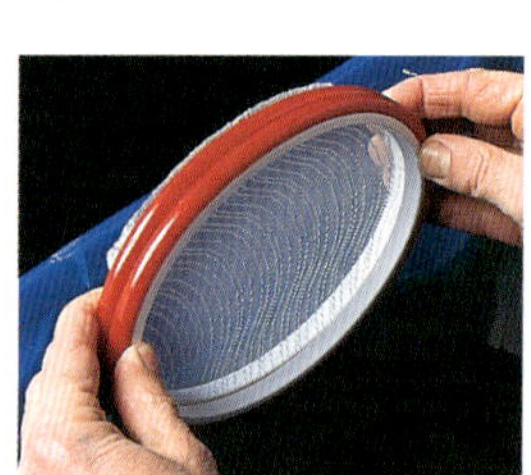

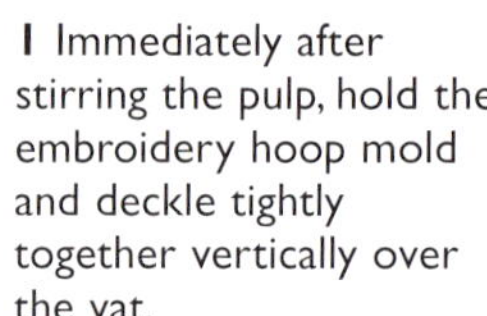

1 Immediately after stirring the pulp, hold the embroidery hoop mold and deckle tightly together vertically over the vat.

2 Follow steps 2–4 of Sheet Forming with a Shaped Mold and Deckle (see page 33).

RIGHT Note the contrast between the whiteness of cotton linters paper (top) and the recycled paper.

It takes a bit of practice to discover the most convenient and comfortable way to hold a shaped mold and deckle when sheet forming, the most important consideration being that they are held together tightly. Using a shaped deckle with the standard mold is a lot easier, although the foamboard deckle still needs to be held firmly against the mesh of the mold to prevent the fibers forming under the deckle. A waterproofed foamboard deckle should prove to be very serviceable.

3 Hold the hoops horizontally in one hand and carefully unscrew the tightening device, if the hoops have one, with the other hand. Lift off the deckle, taking care not to let any water drip onto the formed sheet of paper. If you do drip water onto the formed sheet, or touch the sheet with the deckle when removing it, follow step 9 of Sheet Forming with Recycled Paper Pulp (see page 30).

Sheet forming with a shaped deckle

YOU WILL NEED

- **Pulp in the vat (see pages 28–29)**
- **Shaped deckle (see page 16) and mold**

1 Immediately after stirring the vat of pulp, hold the shaped deckle tightly against the mesh of the mold vertically over the vat.

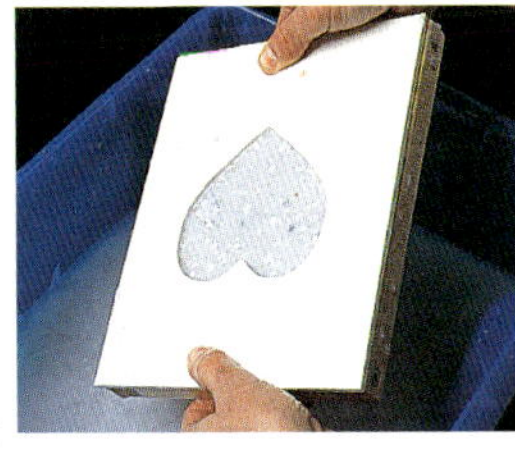

2 Follow steps 2–4 of Sheet Forming with a Shaped Mold and Deckle (see page 33).

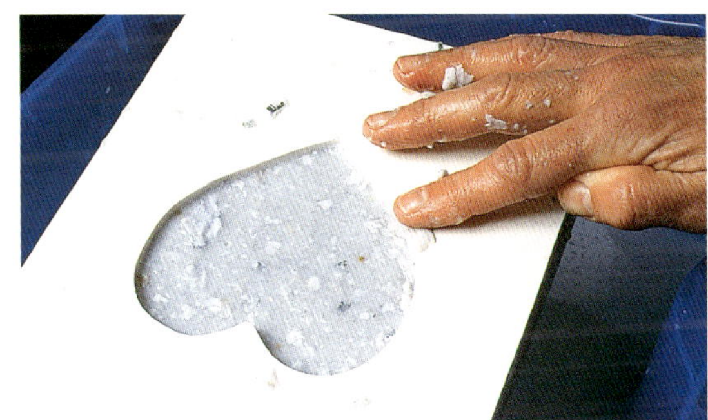

3 If there are surplus bits of pulp around the edge of the deckle shape, carefully remove these so that the shape is not damaged when the deckle is removed.

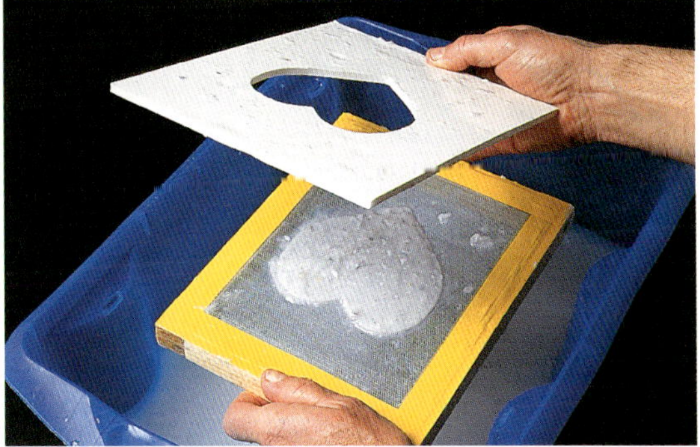

4 Hold the mold horizontally in one hand and lift off the shaped deckle, taking care not to let any water drip onto the formed, shaped sheet of paper. If you do drip water onto the formed sheet, or touch the sheet with the deckle when removing it, follow step 9 of Sheet Forming with Recycled Paper Pulp (see page 30).

Couching

Couching (it rhymes with smooching) is the term used to describe the technique of transferring the formed sheet of paper from the mold to a flat surface. Multiple sheets form a post (stack) of paper prior to pressing.

The first stage in the couching process is to form a couching mound. This is an evenly graduated slope made from wet felts (cloths that are also used to separate each sheet). The couching mound is the vital ingredient in encouraging the formed sheet to leave the mold.

ABOVE *Part-processed pulp was cast on plastic modeling paste before being colored with paint and pencil.*

Couching with a standard mold and deckle

YOU WILL NEED

- **Deckle**
- **Press (see page 17)**
- **Waterproof tape**
- **10 x 8 in (25 x 20cm) blanket**
- **Felts (disposable dishcloths)**
- **Bulldog clips**
- **Shallow tray**
- **2 lengths of 2 x 2 in (5 x 5cm) wood, to fit in the shallow tray**
- **Formed sheet on the mold (see pages 28–33)**

1 Centrally place the deckle on the base board of the press. Stick a length of waterproof tape onto the press board aligning with the bottom edge of the deckle, and a shorter piece on either side. These are the registration marks, used later to line up the mold.

2 Remove the deckle. Lay a 10 x 8 in (25 x 20cm) blanket centrally on the press board within the registration marks.

3 To create a couching mound, wet a felt and fold it three times to create a small, thick shape. Position this centrally on the blanket. Fold a second wet felt three times and lay it on top of the first. Fold a third wet felt twice, and lay this on top of the other two.

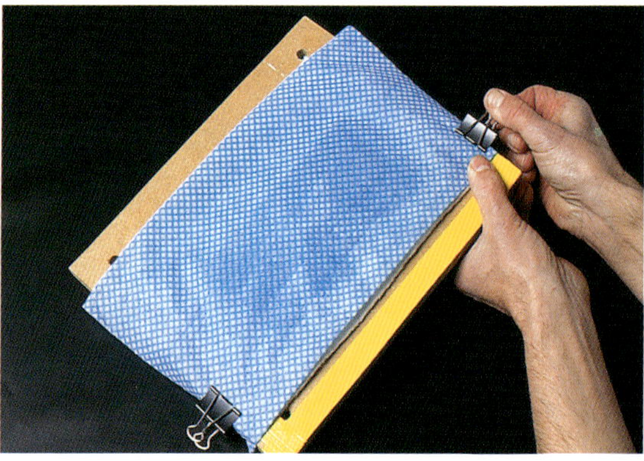

4 Fold a dry felt in half and place it on top of the wet mound. Hold this in place with bulldog clips at each side.

5 To make couching easier, place the press board and couching mound on top of two lengths of wood in a shallow tray that will collect the water.

***RIGHT** To obtain the variations in color and texture, the artist used a mixture of recycled pulp and bracken pulp.*

The most important aspect of the couching technique is that it needs to be done in one continuous movement. It may look tricky but, believe me, it is not, and in no time at all you will become proficient at it.

Although the procedure for couching a formed sheet from a shaped mold is identical to usual couching, there is an extra important consideration: the size and shape of the couching mound should correspond to that of the shaped mold. With some shapes you may find it necessary to make another registration mark on the press board, but remember that the mound must still be positioned where

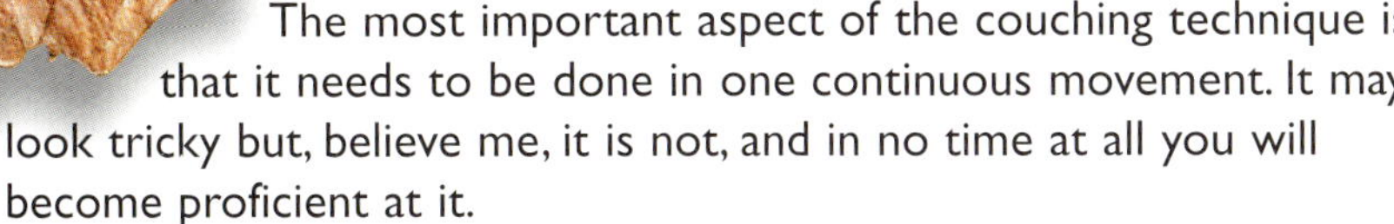

6 Hold the mold, with a formed sheet on it, tilted slightly toward you, on the press board, aligning its edges with the registration marks and with the side holding the sheet of paper facing the rest of the board.

7 Try to work in one continuous movement. Bring the mold up into a vertical position. Keeping the bottom of the mold in position on the registration marks, turn the mold through 180°, bringing it down onto the couching mound. Press down firmly.

8 Continue by moving the mold up into a vertical position on the opposite side of the press board. The formed sheet is left on the couching mound.

9 Lay a dry felt carefully over the formed sheet and hold it in place with the bulldog clips. You can now couch more sheets in the same way.

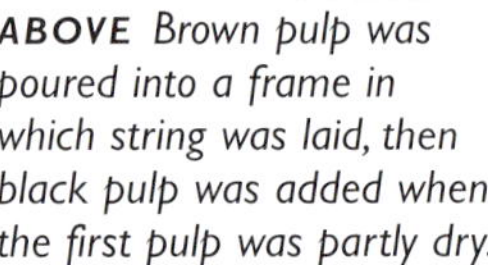

ABOVE *Brown pulp was poured into a frame in which string was laid, then black pulp was added when the first pulp was partly dry.*

the center of the sheet will fall. This registration mark is obviously important as it will ensure that the shaped sheets are couched evenly on top of one another. When using a shaped deckle only this problem does not arise.

As illustrated below, when using the triangular mold it is easier to change direction when bringing the mold off the couching mound. It is a bit more tricky with the embroidery hoop mold, but with a bit of practice you will be able to follow through and complete the couching in one continuous movement as with the standard mold.

Couching with a shaped mold and deckle

YOU WILL NEED

- **Shaped deckle**
- **Press (see page 17)**
- **Waterproof tape**
- **10 x 8 in (25 x 20cm) blanket**
- **Shallow tray**
- **2 lengths of 2 x 2 in (5 x 5cm) wood, to fit in the shallow tray**
- **Felts (disposable dishcloths)**
- **Bulldog clips**
- **Formed sheet on the shaped mold (see page 33)**

1 Follow steps 1 and 2 of Couching with a Standard Mold and Deckle (see page 36).

2 Place the press board on top of two lengths of wood in a shallow tray that will collect the water.

3 Position the deckle on the blanket, lining it up with the registration marks. Make a couching mound in the center of the deckle shape, following step 3 of Couching with a Standard Mold and Deckle (see page 36).

4 Remove the deckle. Fold a dry felt in half, place it on top of the wet mound and smooth it down.

5 Align the shaped mold, tilted slightly toward you, with the registration marks and the side holding the sheet of paper facing the rest of the board.

6 Try to work in one continuous movement. Bring the mold up into a vertical position. Keeping the bottom of the mold on the registration marks, turn it through 180°, bringing it down onto the couching mound. Press down firmly.

7 Continue by moving the mold up into a vertical position on the right-hand side of the press board. The formed sheet is left on the couching mound.

8 Lay a dry felt carefully over the formed sheet. You can now couch more sheets on top of the first in the same way.

Pressing and drying

Pressing and drying are the most straightforward aspects of the sheet-forming process. Pressing a post (stack) of paper expels the last remaining water and helps the fibers in the paper sheets to bond. Sheets are then dried on their felts (disposable dishcloths), otherwise, if left to dry naturally on their own, they will shrink and buckle. The formed sheets adhere quite happily to the felt so the two can be moved about easily without causing any damage to the sheet.

RIGHT
Recycled pulp was used to create this delicately crafted paper.

Using the press

YOU WILL NEED

- **Post (stack) of paper on the pressing board (see pages 36–37)**
- **Felt (disposable dishcloth)**
- **10 x 8 in (25 x 20cm) blanket**
- **Press (see page 17)**

1 When you have a post of paper sheets on the pressing board, cover the last sheet with a dry felt and another 10 x 8 in (25 x 20cm) blanket. Push the bolts of the press up through the holes in the bottom press board.

2 Lower the top press board onto the bolts, and screw on the wing nuts.

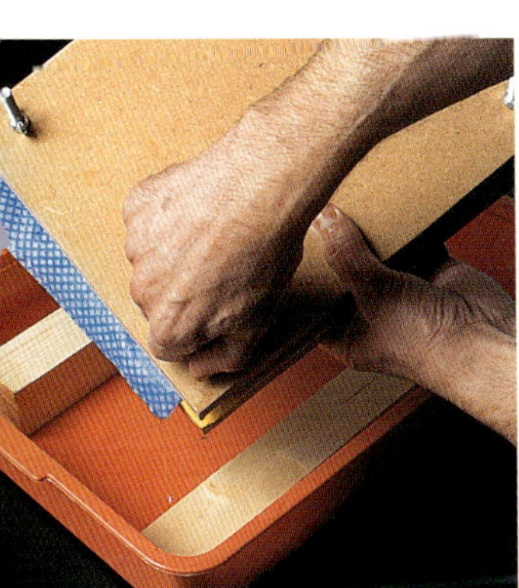

3 Gradually and evenly tighten the nuts, increasing the pressure on the post of paper so that the water is pressed out of the sheets. Do not worry, the pressure will not damage the sheets in any way.

Alternative presses

G-clamps Using G-clamps to put pressure on a post of paper between two pieces of fiberboard is an efficient way to press it. The only drawback with this method is that there is a danger that you could dislodge the post (stack) of paper as the G-clamps are put in position.

Bricks Heavy weights, such as bricks, on top of a post of paper between two pieces of fiberboard, can also be used to press it, although this is a relatively slow method.

Book press By far the best press for a post (stack) of paper between two pieces of fiberboard is a book press, if you are lucky enough to have access to one.

Whether hung up or left to dry flat, where you choose to dry your sheets of paper is an important consideration. Ideally, the warmer the environment the better, so paper left to dry in a warm domestic environment will dry more quickly than paper left to dry in the garage.

Alternatively, sheets can be left outside on a sunny day, either flat or hung up, though you may find impurities are blown onto the sheets by the wind, or that insects land on them. Although hanging sheets out to dry on a windy

Hanging sheets to dry

YOU WILL NEED

- **Pressed post (stack) of paper (see pages 36–39)**
- **Clothes hanging line**
- **Clothes pegs**
- **Shallow tray**

1 Carefully lift the first formed sheet, on its felt (disposable dishcloth), off the post.

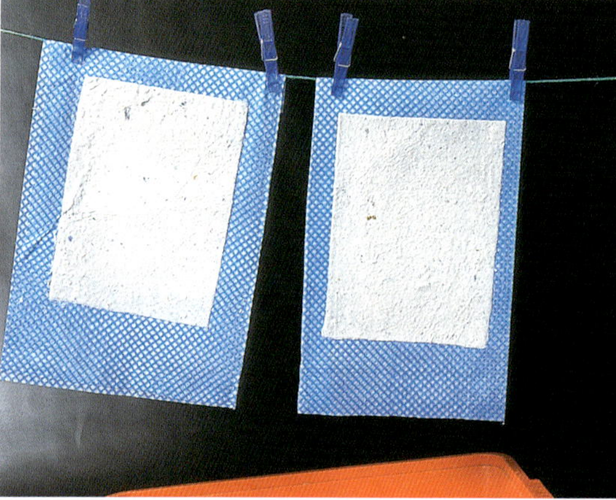

2 Hang the felt with the sheet attached onto a clothes line. If you are drying inside you may find it useful to put a tray underneath to collect the drips of water. Hang out all the sheets, with their felts, in the same way.

3 Once dry, the sheet can easily be lifted off the felt. Note that paper dried in this way tends to buckle.

Drying sheets on melamine

YOU WILL NEED

- **Pressed post (stack) of paper (see pages 36–39)**
- **Melamine sheet**
- **Paintbrush**
- **Roller**
- **Iron (optional)**
- **Flexible palette knife**

1 Carefully lift the top sheet and felt (disposable dishcloth) off the post.

2 Lay the felt with the sheet face down on a melamine surface. With a dry paintbrush, carefully brush the sheet down, through the felt, onto the melamine, working from the center to the sides.

LEFT AND RIGHT *From a series of pieces relating to pregnancy and childbirth entitled "Mammacord." The artist uses a variety of methods, including embedding and embossing.*

day may seem like a good idea, I wouldn't advise it. The sheets have a tendency to blow off their felts (disposable dishcloths), forcing you to chase them around the garden. Another efficient method to hang dry sheets is to peg them to a radiator. This makes the drying time very quick, but it can produce a particularly buckled sheet of paper.

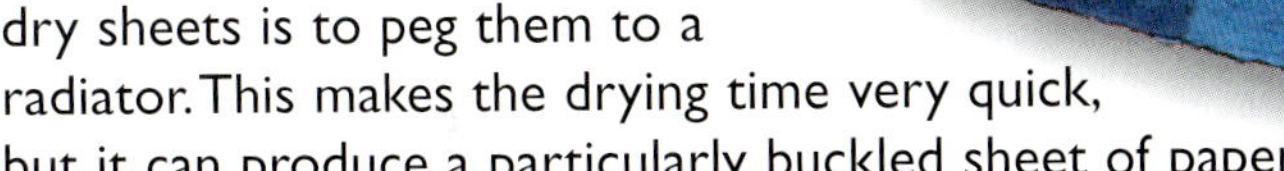

3 Work a roller over the felt, pressing the sheet firmly onto the melamine. Slowly peel off the felt. Transfer the remaining sheets to the melamine in the same way.

4 Leave the sheets to dry on the melamine in a warm environment, for about a week.

6 Use a flexible palette knife to gently tease and lift up the edges of a sheet. Once you have lifted one corner you will be able to gently peel the rest of the sheet away.

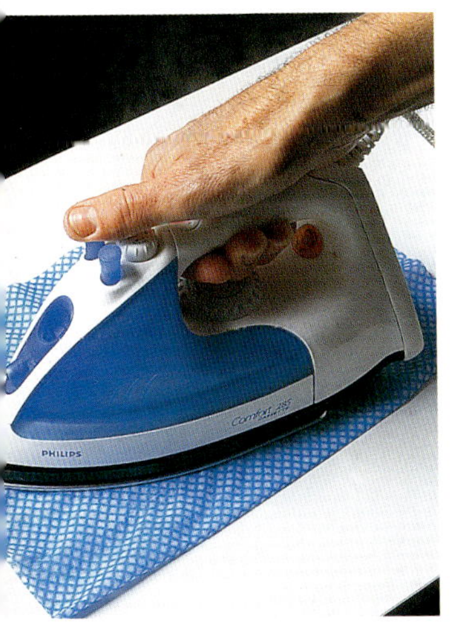

5 Alternatively, at this stage you can speed up the melamine drying process using an iron. Do not remove the felt. Carefully iron over the felt, frequently looking under it to see if the sheet is dry.

The melamine drying process produces sheets with particularly smooth undersides.

Making laminated papers

Once you have become proficient at making sheets of paper, learning the laminating technique is the natural first step in increasing your papermaking skills. This technique allows you to make a thicker and therefore stronger sheet of paper. It relies on couching one formed sheet on top of another—followed by pressing and drying—enabling the fibers in both sheets to interlock and bond together into one homogeneous mass, therefore forming one sheet. You will soon learn that the registration marks on the press board prove to be

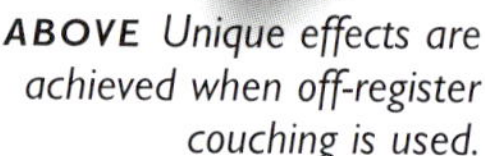

ABOVE *Unique effects are achieved when off-register couching is used.*

Two-tone laminated paper

YOU WILL NEED

- **Kraft pulp in the vat (see pages 22–23 and 28)**
- **Mold and deckle**
- **Press prepared for couching (see pages 36–37)**
- **Cotton linters pulp in the vat (see pages 22–23 and 30)**
- **Felts (disposable dishcloths)**
- **10 x 8 in (25 x 20cm) blanket**
- **Melamine sheet**
- **Paintbrush**
- **Roller**
- **Iron (optional)**
- **Flexible palette knife**

1 Form and couch a sheet of kraft pulp paper (see pages 28–29 and 36–37), but do not cover it with a felt.

2 Form a sheet of cotton linters paper and align the mold with the registration marks of the press board.

3 Couch the second sheet. Using the registration marks ensures that the second sheet falls directly on top of the first.

4 Lay a dry felt on top of the sheets. Build up a post (stack) in the same way, if required. Press in the normal way (see page 39).

5 Use the melamine board drying method (see page 40), pulling back the felt occasionally to check if the sheet is dry.

6 Once dry, carefully lift up the sheet to reveal the white of the other side of what has now become one sheet of paper.

indispensable for this technique. Alternatively, you can dispense with the use of registration marks and create an interesting shaped laminated sheet using off-register couching.

You may find that your mold is not large enough to make the size of sheet you require. Don't despair, there are two laminating methods you can employ to make larger sheets from smaller ones. Success still depends on the laminating principle, except that in this case it is the pressure of the roller that bonds the fibers of the sheets together.

ABOVE *Laminated, multi-colored recycled pulp paper was hand-placed on the mold, off register.*

Off-register couching

YOU WILL NEED

- **Plant fiber pulp in the vat (see pages 24–27)**
- **Mold and deckle**
- **Press prepared for couching (see pages 36–37)**
- **Recycled paper pulp in the vat (see pages 20–21 and 28)**
- **Felts (disposable dishcloths)**
- **10 x 8 in (25 x 20cm) blanket**
- **Melamine sheet**
- **Paintbrush**
- **Roller**
- **Iron (optional)**
- **Flexible palette knife**

1 Form and couch a sheet of plant pulp paper diagonally across the couching mound (see pages 30–31 and 36–37). Do not cover with a felt.

2 Form and couch a recycled paper pulp sheet diagonally across the plant fiber sheet.

3 Form and couch another plant pulp sheet on top of the recycled paper sheet at a variance to its diagonal, so as not to obscure it completely.

4 Lay a dry felt on top of the three sheets. Build up a post (stack) in the same way, if required. Press in the normal way (see page 39).

5 Use the melamine board drying method (see page 40), working over the felt with the roller a second time to make sure the fibers are matted together.

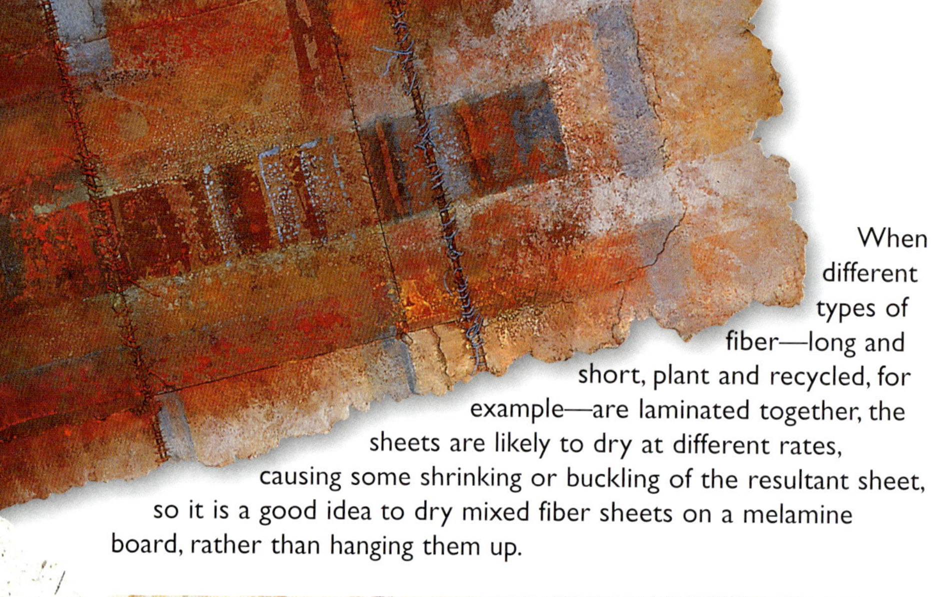

When different types of fiber—long and short, plant and recycled, for example—are laminated together, the sheets are likely to dry at different rates, causing some shrinking or buckling of the resultant sheet, so it is a good idea to dry mixed fiber sheets on a melamine board, rather than hanging them up.

***LEFT** Cotton linters pulp was used for this beautifully colored piece, which was laminated, sized, cut, and then stitched before being painted and waxed.*

Making a large sheet

YOU WILL NEED

- **Cotton linters pulp in the vat (see pages 22–23 and 28)**
- **Mold and deckle**
- **Press prepared for couching (see pages 36–37)**
- **Felts (disposable dishcloths)**
- **Melamine sheet**
- **Paintbrush**
- **Roller**
- **Iron (optional)**
- **Flexible palette knife**

1 Form and couch four sheets of cotton linters pulp, separated by felts (see pages 30–31 and 36–37). Lightly press as usual (see page 39).

2 Remove the first sheet from the post (stack), still on its felt, and lay it face down on a melamine sheet. With a dry paintbrush, carefully brush the sheet down, through the felt, onto the melamine, working from the center out to the sides. Remove the felt.

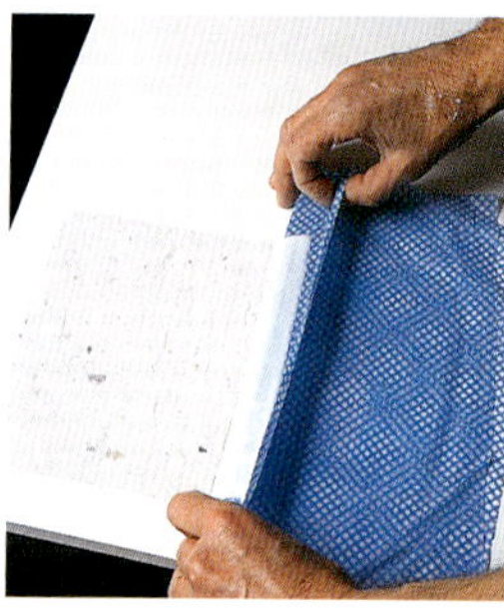

3 Transfer the next sheet to the melamine in the same way, carefully positioning it so that its longest edge overlaps the longest edge of the previous sheet by ¾ in (2cm). This laying down operation is done completely by eye, so don't worry too much if the two sheets do not exactly line up.

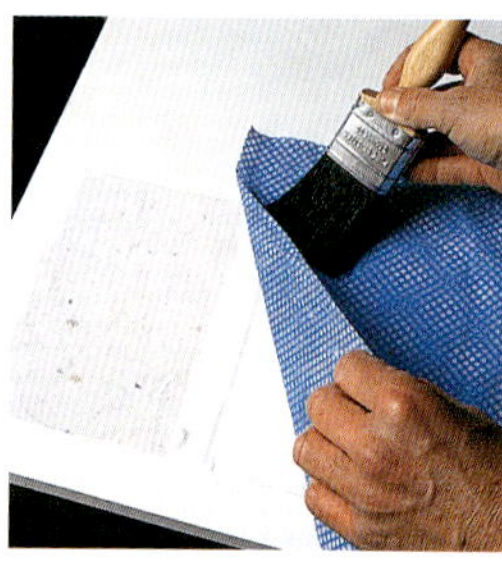

4 Brush the second sheet down onto the melamine and lift off the felt.

5 Lay down the third sheet, overlapping its shortest edge to the short edge of the first sheet by ¾ in (2cm). Brush and remove the felt as usual.

6 Lay down the fourth sheet, this time overlapping the shortest edge with the short edge of the second sheet and the longest edge with the long edge of the third sheet, again by ¾ in (2cm). Brush and remove the felt.

7 Cover the large sheet with a dry felt and carefully work over the whole sheet with a roller, providing firm and even pressure and paying particular attention to the overlapping joints. These will need to be pressed well down.

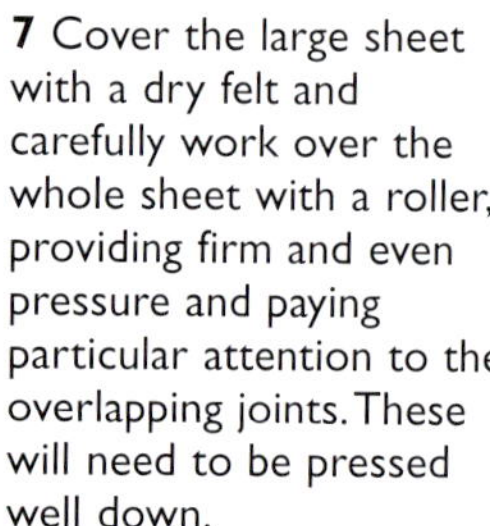

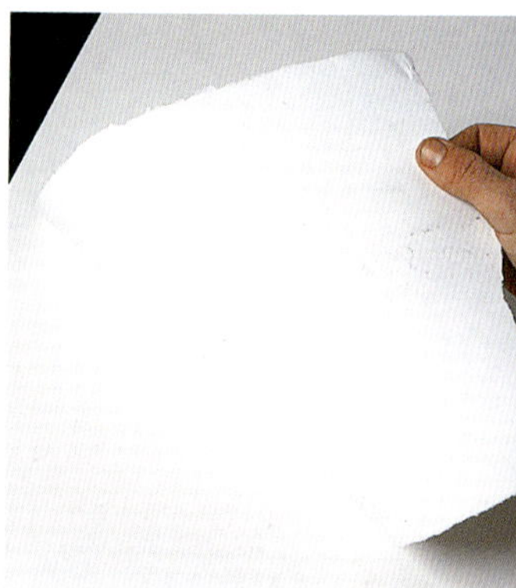

8 Leave the sheet to dry, or iron it (see steps 4–5, page 41). When dry, use a flexible palette knife to lift up the edges, then carefully pull the whole sheet away from the melamine. The four formed sheets have now become one larger sheet.

LEFT A large sheet can be made with sheets of the same pulp, but different pulps give an interesting effect.

Although standard-shaped sheets are used in these techniques, you could also use shaped papers to create all manner of wonderful new designs using combinations of shaped papers and different pulps.

Using different pulps to make a large sheet

YOU WILL NEED

- **Cotton linters pulp in the vat (see pages 22–23 and 28)**
- **Mold and deckle**
- **Press prepared for couching (see pages 36–37)**
- **Felts (disposable dishcloths)**
- **Recycled paper pulp in the vat (see pages 20–21 and 28)**
- **Plant fiber pulp in the vat (see pages 24–27 and 28)**
- **Melamine sheet**
- **Paintbrush**
- **Roller**
- **Iron (optional)**
- **Flexible palette knife**

1 Form and couch a sheet each of cotton linters, recycled paper, and plant fiber pulp, separated by felts (see pages 28–32 and 36–37). Lightly press them as usual (see page 39).

2 Remove the plant fiber sheet from the post (stack), still on its felt, and lay it face down on a melamine sheet. With a dry paintbrush, carefully brush the sheet down, through the felt, onto the melamine, working from the center out to the sides. Remove the felt.

3 Transfer the recycled paper sheet to the melamine in the same way, carefully positioning it so that its longest edge overlaps the longest edge of the previous sheet by ¾ in (2cm). Because this laying down operation is done completely by eye, the two sheets may not exactly line up.

4 Brush the second sheet down onto the melamine and lift off the felt.

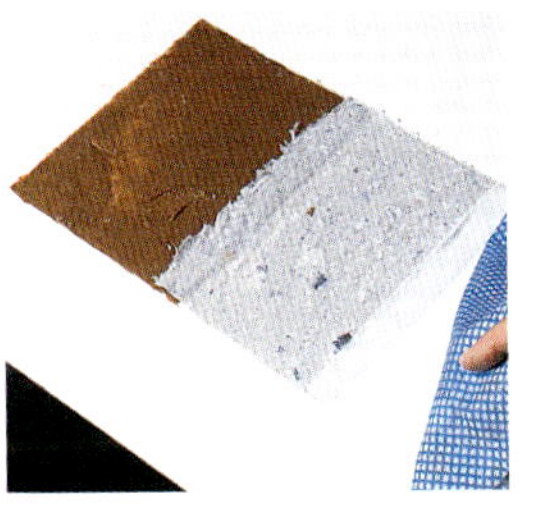

5 Finally, lay down the cotton linters sheet, overlapping its longest edge to the long edge of the recycled paper sheet by ¾ in (2cm). Brush and remove the felt as usual.

6 Lay a dry felt over the three sheets and work over them with a roller with firm, even pressure, paying special attention to the overlapping joints that must be pressed down well.

7 Leave the sheet to dry, or iron it (see steps 4–5, page 41). When dry, use a flexible palette knife to lift up the edges, then carefully pull the whole sheet away from the melamine. The three sheets have now become one, but with three different sections of color.

Embedded papers

An embedded sheet of paper contains additional material held in place by the fibers of the pulp. There are two methods of embedding material. The first uses the laminating technique, its advantage being that you have complete control over the positioning of the material to be embedded. You can then either leave the material embedded in the paper or create an interesting effect by removing it. The other method of embedding is to add the material to

***ABOVE** Here, a simple pattern has been created with pipe cleaners.*

Embedding a wire pattern

YOU WILL NEED

- **Pipe cleaners**
- **Scissors**
- **Cotton linters pulp in the vat (see pages 22–23 and 28)**
- **Mold and deckle**
- **Press prepared for couching (see pages 36–37)**
- **Felts (disposable dishcloths)**
- **10 x 8 in (25 x 20cm) blanket**
- **Melamine sheet**
- **Paintbrush**
- **Roller**
- **Iron (optional)**
- **Flexible palette knife**

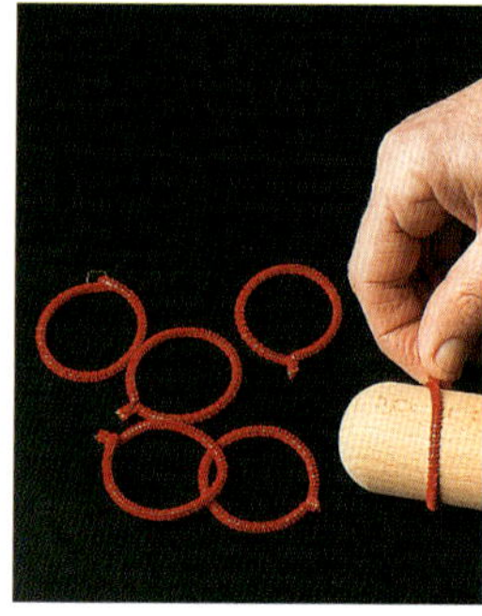

1 Bend a pipe cleaner around a rolling pin. Twist the ends of the pipe cleaner together twice and cut off the excess. Make six of these shapes.

2 Form and couch a sheet of cotton linters paper (see pages 28–31 and 36–37). Place the pipe-cleaner circles equidistant to one another in two rows on the sheet, leaving a 1 in (2.5cm) margin all the way around.

3 Using the registration marks on the press board, couch another sheet of cotton linters paper on top of the first sheet and the circles.

4 Lay a dry felt on top of both sheets. Build up a post (stack) in the same way, if required. Press in the usual way (see page 39), then dry on a melamine board (see page 40).

RIGHT Entitled "Early Spring," this piece was made with cotton linters pulp embedded with petals.

the pulp in the vat prior to forming a sheet. The characteristic of this method is that you have no control over the positioning of the embedded material, so every sheet you produce is unique. Remember that while we have specified the pulps used in each technique, you can embed any material in any pulp.

Embedding dried flowers

YOU WILL NEED

- **Dried flowers**
- **Bowl of water**
- **Cotton linters pulp in the vat (see pages 22–23 and 28)**
- **Mold and deckle**
- **Press prepared for couching (see pages 36–37)**
- **Felts (disposable dishcloths)**
- **10 x 8 in (25 x 20cm) blanket**
- **Melamine sheet**
- **Paintbrush**
- **Roller**
- **Iron (optional)**
- **Flexible palette knife**

BELOW Careful positioning of the dried flowers on the paper creates an instant work of art.

1 Soak the dried flowers in a bowl of water for 30 minutes.

3 Using the registration marks on the press board, couch another sheet of cotton linters paper directly on top of the first sheet and the flowers, taking care not to dislodge the flowers.

2 Form and couch a sheet of cotton linters paper (see pages 30–31 and 36–37). Arrange the flowers centrally on the sheet of paper in a design of your choice.

4 Lay a dry felt on top of both sheets. Build up a post (stack) if required, then press in the normal way (see page 39).

5 Dry on a melamine board (see page 40).

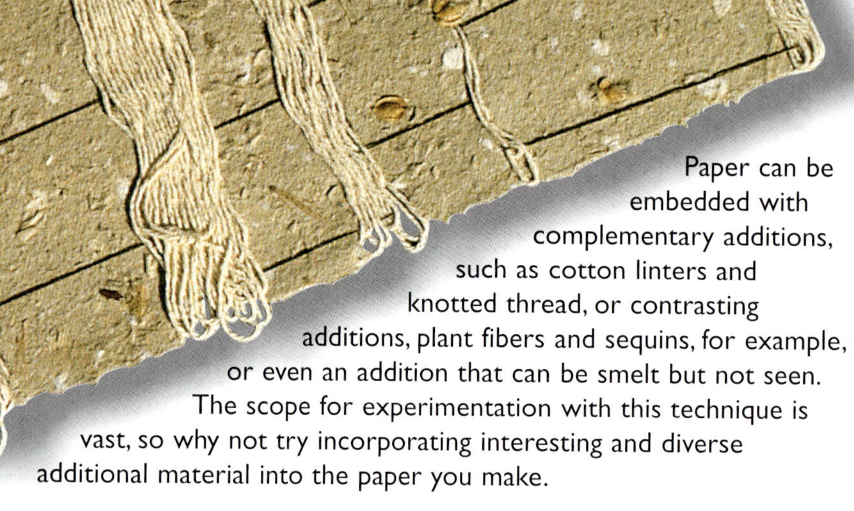

Paper can be embedded with complementary additions, such as cotton linters and knotted thread, or contrasting additions, plant fibers and sequins, for example, or even an addition that can be smelt but not seen. The scope for experimentation with this technique is vast, so why not try incorporating interesting and diverse additional material into the paper you make.

LEFT *The artist has used recycled newspaper and cartridge paper embedded with seed heads and cotton.*

Embedding and removing string to create a torn surface

YOU WILL NEED

- **Kraft pulp in the vat (see pages 22–23)**
- **Mold and deckle**
- **Press prepared for couching (see pages 36–37)**
- **Felts (disposable dishcloths)**
- **Cotton linters pulp in the vat (see pages 22–23 and 28)**
- **10 x 8 in (25 x 20cm) blanket**
- **Melamine sheet**
- **Paintbrush**
- **Double-sided adhesive tape**
- **Scissors**
- **String**
- **Roller**
- **Iron (optional)**
- **Flexible palette knife**

1 Form and couch a cotton linters sheet and a kraft one, separated by felts (see pages 30–32 and 36–37). Lightly press them as usual (see page 39).

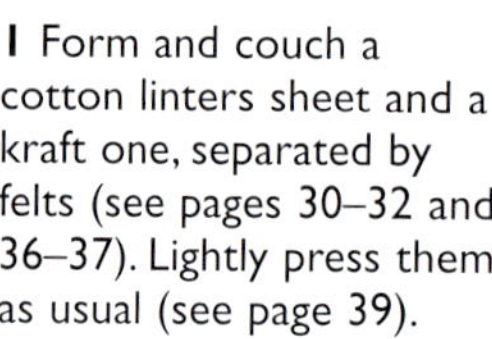

2 Remove the kraft sheet from the post (stack), still on its felt, and lay it face down on a melamine sheet. With a dry paintbrush, carefully brush the sheet down, through the felt, onto the melamine, working from the center out to the sides. Remove the felt.

3 Fix a length of double-sided adhesive tape 2 in (5cm) from each of the two short edges of the sheet. Remove the tape's backing paper.

4 Cut five 12 in (30cm) lengths of string. You now need to lay the string lengths, equally spaced apart, along the length of the sheet. Fix one end of a string length to one of the adhesive tape strips. Pull the string taut along the length of the sheet and stick the other end to the opposite tape strip.

When embedding, keep in mind the final use of the paper. Is it going to be functional or decorative? Using the laminating technique enables you to embed large and bulky objects, but the resultant paper is only suitable for decorative use—you will not be able to write on it.

These bulky embedded papers can look very attractive in picture frames, or alternatively they could be used to decorate the cover of a scrap book or box lid. You could even stick a small magnet on the back to create a paper fridge magnet.

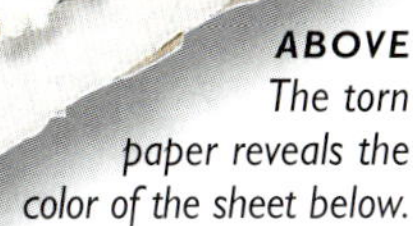

ABOVE *The torn paper reveals the color of the sheet below.*

5 Take up the cotton linters sheet on its felt, and carefully position its longest edge along the longest edge of the laid sheet. Once in position, lay the second sheet down directly on top of the first and the string.

6 Open out the felt and work over the whole sheet with a roller, using firm, even pressure including in the spaces between the lengths of string.

7 Remove the felt and carefully pull the strings along the length of the sheet. Guide the string with your fingers.

8 Leave the sheet to dry, or iron it (see steps 4–5, page 41). When dry, use a flexible palette knife to lift up the edges, then carefully pull the whole sheet away from the melamine. A very attractive torn edge is created, revealing the color and texture of the sheet of paper below.

An attractive greeting card can be made by simply folding a sheet of handmade paper in half and then sticking an embedded paper on the front. You could be more adventurous with the first technique, illustrated on page 46, and bend the wire into a more specific shape, such as the outline of a face, a dog or cat, or even a name. The resultant paper would make an attractive name plaque that could be hung on the door of a bedroom.

ABOVE *Spice seeds add a touch of exotic color to embedded papers.*

Adding seeds to recycled paper pulp

YOU WILL NEED

- **Selection of spice seeds**
- **Bowl**
- **Recycled paper pulp in the vat (see pages 20–21 and 28)**
- **Wooden implement for stirring**
- **Mold and deckle**
- **Press prepared for couching (see pages 36–37)**
- **Felts (disposable dishcloths)**
- **10 x 8 in (25 x 20cm) blanket**
- **Melamine sheet**
- **Paintbrush**
- **Roller**
- **Iron (optional)**
- **Flexible palette knife**

1 Empty a selection of spice seeds into a bowl and mix well together. Try to choose seeds for variety of color and size.

2 Empty the seeds into the vat of recycled paper pulp and give it a good stir to make sure the seeds are evenly distributed around the vat.

3 Form a sheet (see pages 28–31). Give the mold and deckle a stronger shake from side to side than usual to make sure that the seeds are evenly dispersed across the surface of the sheet.

4 Carefully couch a sheet or post (stack) of sheets (see pages 36–37).

5 Press in the normal way (see page 39) and dry on a melamine board (see page 40).

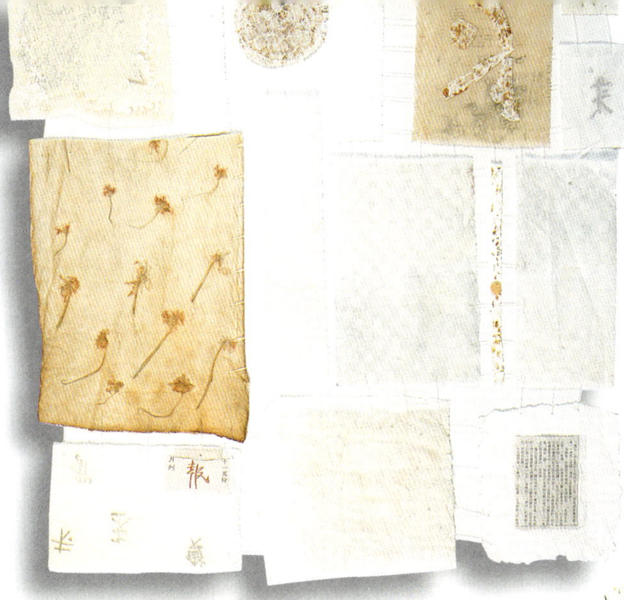

If you want to make an embedded paper that can be written or painted on, then you will need to choose an embedding material that is as unobtrusive as possible. Seeds are a good choice, although they need to be as small as possible, or try confetti or tea leaves.

RIGHT AND BELOW LEFT *Delicately colored papers embedded with petals, flowers, fibers, thread, and stitching.*

Adding knotted thread to cotton linters pulp

YOU WILL NEED

- **6 in (15cm) lengths of thread**
- **Bowl of water**
- **Cotton linters pulp in the vat (see pages 22–23 and 28)**
- **Wooden implement for stirring**
- **Mold and deckle**
- **Press prepared for couching (see pages 36–37)**
- **Felts (disposable dishcloths)**
- **10 x 8 in (25 x 20cm) blanket**
- **Melamine sheet**
- **Paintbrush**
- **Roller**
- **Iron (optional)**
- **Flexible palette knife**

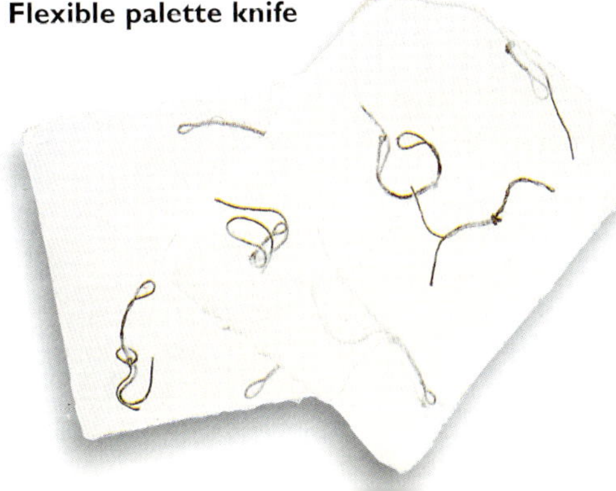

1 Loop the threads and knot them at the end. Soak them in a bowl of water for 15 minutes. This will prevent them floating on the surface of the pulp and water mixture in the vat.

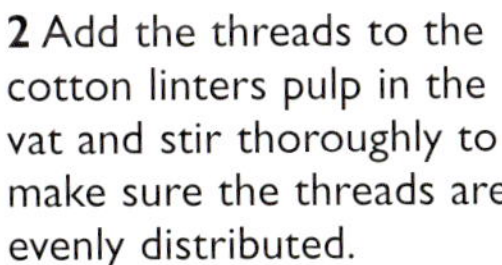

2 Add the threads to the cotton linters pulp in the vat and stir thoroughly to make sure the threads are evenly distributed.

3 When the threads are dispersed around the vat, form a sheet (see pages 28–31).

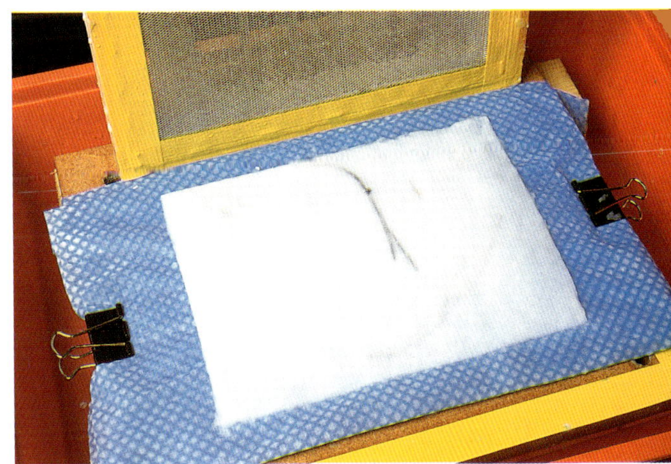

4 Couch a sheet or post (stack) of sheets (see pages 36–37).

5 Press in the normal way (see page 39) and dry on a melamine board (see page 40).

LEFT Recycled pulp was embedded with threads directly on the mold.

When embedding any plant material, whether dried flowers or seeds, there is always the likelihood that some coloring will bleed from the embedded material into the formed sheet of paper. Such random coloring should be seen as a positive virtue, this unpredictability being one of the most exciting things about papermaking.

ABOVE The plant fiber pulp offers an interesting contrast to the embedded sequins.

Adding sequins to plant fiber pulp

YOU WILL NEED

- **Sequin material**
- **Scissors**
- **Bowl**
- **Plant fiber pulp in the vat (see pages 24–27)**
- **Wooden implement for stirring**
- **Mold and deckle**
- **Press prepared for couching (see pages 36–37)**
- **Felts (disposable dishcloths)**
- **10 x 8 in (25 x 20cm) blanket**
- **Melamine sheet**
- **Paintbrush**
- **Roller**
- **Iron (optional)**
- **Flexible palette knife**

1 Cut some sequin material into manageably sized pieces: pieces that are too large may hinder the making of the sheet of paper.

2 Empty the cut sequins into the vat of plant fiber pulp and evenly disperse the material.

3 Form a sheet (see pages 28–30). Give the mold and deckle a stronger shake from side to side than usual to make sure that the sequins are evenly dispersed across the surface of the sheet.

4 Couch a sheet or post (stack) of sheets (see pages 36–37).

5 Press in the normal way (see page 39) and dry on a melamine board (see page 40).

ABOVE *Embedded plastic strips create a work of art. There is no limit to the colors you can use.*

Adding plastic strips to plant fiber pulp

YOU WILL NEED

- Craft knife
- Metal ruler
- Cutting mat
- Plastic shopping bags, of different colors
- Scissors
- Plant fiber pulp in the vat (see pages 24–27)
- Wooden implement for stirring
- Mold and deckle
- Press prepared for couching (see pages 36–37)
- Felts (disposable dishcloths)
- 10 x 8 in (25 x 20cm) blanket
- Melamine sheet
- Paintbrush
- Roller
- Iron (optional)
- Flexible palette knife

1 Use a craft knife and metal ruler on a cutting mat to trim ¼ in (0.5cm) strips of plastic bag. Cut these strips into 2 in (5cm) lengths.

2 Sprinkle the plastic lengths, which may float to begin with, into the vat of plant fiber pulp. Stir well to disperse the strips in the pulp.

3 Form a sheet (see pages 28–31). You will probably pick up the strips on the side of the deckle as you pull it out. Quickly brush these off before removing the deckle.

4 Couch a sheet or post (stack) of sheets (see pages 36–37), stirring the plastic strips before you form each new sheet.

5 Press in the normal way (see page 39) and dry on a melamine board (see page 40).

LEFT Pine needles provide a dramatic effect against the white cotton linters pulp.

Why not try out combinations of embedding and laminating to create really interesting shaped and textured papers. The effect of light seen through an embedded paper is stunning, and it is possible to use embedded papers to make a lampshade or to fix a variety of embedded papers to a window for an

RIGHT The addition of perfume to paper embedded with petals increases its romantic appeal.

Adding pine needles to cotton linters pulp

YOU WILL NEED

- **Saucepan**
- **Scissors**
- **Pine branch**
- **Strainer**
- **Net curtain fabric**
- **Cotton linters pulp in the vat (see pages 22–23 and 28)**
- **Wooden implement for stirring**
- **Mold and deckle**
- **Press prepared for couching (see pages 36–37)**
- **Felts (disposable dishcloths)**
- **10 x 8 in (25 x 20cm) blanket**
- **Melamine sheet**
- **Paintbrush**
- **Roller**
- **Iron (optional)**
- **Flexible palette knife**

1 Part fill a saucepan with water and cut ½ in (1.5cm) lengths off a pine branch into the water. Some of the needles will also naturally fall off into the water. To get rid of any impurities, boil the needles for 15 minutes.

2 Drain the boiled needles into a strainer lined with net curtain fabric. Rinse well.

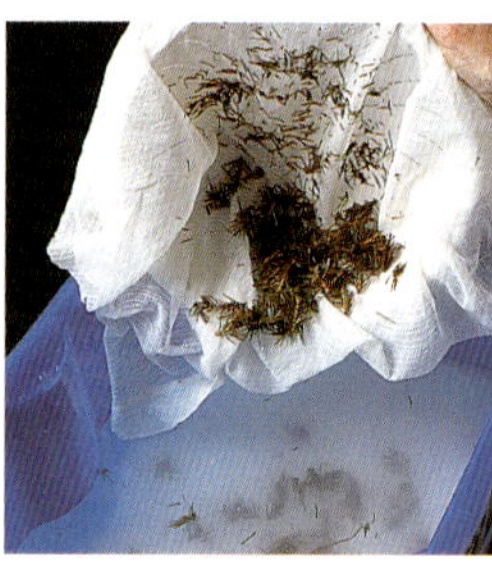

3 Empty the needles into the vat of cotton linters pulp and stir thoroughly until evenly distributed.

4 Form a sheet (see pages 28–31). Give the mold and deckle a stronger shake from side to side than usual to make sure that the material is evenly dispersed across the surface of the sheet.

5 Couch a sheet or post (stack) of sheets (see pages 36–37).

6 Press in the normal way (see page 39) and dry on a melamine board (see page 40).

attractive backlit effect. For the more adventurous papermaker, embedded papers can be used as the panels of a screen, or a dreary coffee table can be brightened up by sticking the paper to the tabletop and covering it with a sheet of thick glass.

ABOVE *Cotton linters and red silk paper have been embedded with petals.*

Adding perfumed oil and petals to cotton linters pulp

YOU WILL NEED

- **Lavender leaves and buds**
- **Bowl of water**
- **Lavender essential oil**
- **Wooden implement for stirring**
- **Cotton linters pulp in the vat (see pages 22–23 and 28)**
- **Mold and deckle**
- **Press prepared for couching (see pages 36–37)**
- **Felts (disposable dishcloths)**
- **10 x 8 in (25 x 20cm) blanket**
- **Melamine sheet**
- **Paintbrush**
- **Roller**
- **Iron (optional)**
- **Flexible palette knife**

1 Add the lavender leaves and buds to a bowl of water, then add a few drops of lavender essential oil. Mix the oil well into the water.

2 Immerse the bowl of leaves and the perfumed water into the vat of cotton linters pulp and let the material float out into the pulp. Stir thoroughly to evenly distribute the leaves and scent.

3 Form a sheet (see pages 28–31). Give the mold and deckle a stronger shake from side to side than usual to make sure that the material is evenly dispersed across the surface of the sheet.

4 Couch a sheet or post (stack) of sheets (see pages 36–37).

5 Press in the normal way (see page 39) and dry on a melamine board (see page 40).

also see the following pages
Making pulp from plant fibers 24–25
Sheet forming: sheet forming with plant fiber pulp 32 • **Couching** 36–37
Pressing 39 • **Making laminated papers: making a large sheet** 44 • **Drying** 40–41

Project 1

Wall hanging

The organic elements in this hanging complement each other wonderfully. The fiber to make the paper comes from wild plant material, while the dried teasels themselves are a wild plant. Alternatively, you could use any thistle head, wheat, or seed pods. Plant pulp is practical, because the long fibers of the paper can grip around the stalks of the teasels.

YOU WILL NEED

- **Scissors**
- **3 dried teasels (or similar dried thistle heads)**
- **3 6 x 8 in (15 x 20cm) lightly pressed sheets of plant fiber paper (see pages 24–25 and 28–39)**
- **Melamine sheet**
- **Paintbrush**
- **Roller**
- **Flexible palette knife**

1 To allow the teasel or thistle to sit flat on the surface of the paper, use a pair of scissors to cut each head in half lengthwise so that half a head remains attached to the stem.

2 Take a sheet of lightly pressed plant fiber paper, still on its felt, and lay it face down on a melamine sheet. With a dry paintbrush, carefully brush the sheet down, through the felt, onto the melamine, working from the center out to the sides. Remove the felt.

3 Position a second sheet of plant fiber paper parallel to the first, so that the long edge of the second sheet overlaps the long edge of the first sheet by ¾ in (2cm).

4 Brush the sheet down flat onto the melamine. Leave the felt in place and firmly roll over the overlap to ensure the fibers of the two sheets bond together. Remove the felt.

5 Place the largest of the teasels in the center of the paper and position the other two diagonally on either side so that the ends of the stalks touch at the bottom of the sheet.

6 Position a third sheet of plant fiber paper lengthwise, centrally overlapping the bottom of the composite sheet—and therefore the stems of the teasels—by 1½ in (4cm).

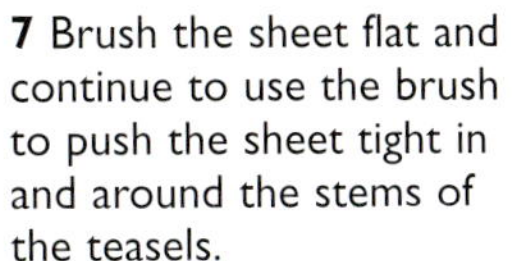

7 Brush the sheet flat and continue to use the brush to push the sheet tight in and around the stems of the teasels.

8 Use the roller to firmly roll over the overlap of the last sheet of paper, working in all directions against the teasel stems.

9 Leave to dry on the melamine sheet. Once dry, gently insert a flexible palette knife under the wall hanging to ease it up from the board. Make sure you lift carefully and evenly all the way around.

Embossed papers

The embossing technique involves making an impression on a sheet of paper with a textured surface, the profile of a shape, or a combination of both. An embossed impression in paper can be achieved by simply pressing a textured object onto the surface of a formed sheet using the pressure of your hand. Alternatively, you can leave the formed sheet on the couching mound and use the press to make the impression.

ABOVE *Cotton linters paper has been embossed over old toaster elements.*

Embossing by hand: using keys

YOU WILL NEED

- **Pressed post (stack) of paper (see pages 36–39), thick sheets are preferable**
- **Melamine sheet**
- **Keys**
- **Clothes hanging line**
- **Clothes pegs**
- **Shallow tray**

1 Transfer a lightly pressed, thick sheet of paper, felt first, onto a melamine sheet.

2 Lay a few keys on top of the sheet and, with your hand, press each one down into the paper as hard as possible.

3 Use a craft knife to lift each key to avoid marking the sheet with fingerprints. Repeat on more sheets of paper if required.

4 Hang the sheets up to dry (see page 40).

Embossing by hand: using a shoe sole

YOU WILL NEED

- **Pressed post (stack) of paper (see pages 36–39), thick sheets are preferable**
- **Melamine sheet**
- **Textured shoe sole**
- **Clothes hanging line**
- **Clothes pegs**
- **Shallow tray**

1 Transfer a lightly pressed, thick sheet of paper, felt first, onto a melamine sheet.

2 Press the sole of a shoe firmly down onto the sheet of paper, taking care not to dislodge the fragile surface of the paper.

3 Carefully lift the sole of the shoe away from the sheet of paper, revealing the texture left on the sheet. Repeat on more sheets of paper if required.

4 Hang the sheets up to dry (see page 40).

RIGHT *The artist cast this cotton linters paper directly onto an old door.*

Whichever technique you use, it is important to form a thick sheet of paper to begin with, so put extra pulp into the vat prior to forming.

Although it is possible to use these embossing techniques with a short fiber plant paper, the most satisfactory results will be obtained using recycled paper or a part-processed pulp such as cotton linters. You could use an embossing technique to personalize a sheet of paper, especially if it is going to be notepaper, in much the same way as using a watermark.

Embossing by hand: using a serrated pen lid

YOU WILL NEED

- Pressed post (stack) of paper (see pages 36–39), thick sheets are preferable
- Melamine sheet
- Serrated pen lid
- Clothes hanging line
- Clothes pegs
- Shallow tray

1 Transfer a lightly pressed sheet of paper, felt first, onto a melamine sheet.

2 Roll a serrated pen lid along each side of the sheet. Repeat on more sheets of paper if required.

3 Hang the sheets up to dry (see page 40).

BELOW *The serrated pen lid gives a subtle ridged effect to the finished paper.*

Embossing with the press: using cutout card shapes

YOU WILL NEED

- Foamboard
- Pencil
- Mold and deckle
- Craft knife
- Cutting mat
- Acrylic varnish
- Paintbrush
- Pulp in the vat (see pages 28–29), of a thick consistency
- Press prepared for couching (see pages 36–37)
- Felts (disposable cloths)
- Several 10 x 8 in (25 x 20cm) blankets
- Clothes hanging line
- Clothes pegs
- Shallow tray

1 Draw around the deckle onto some foamboard.

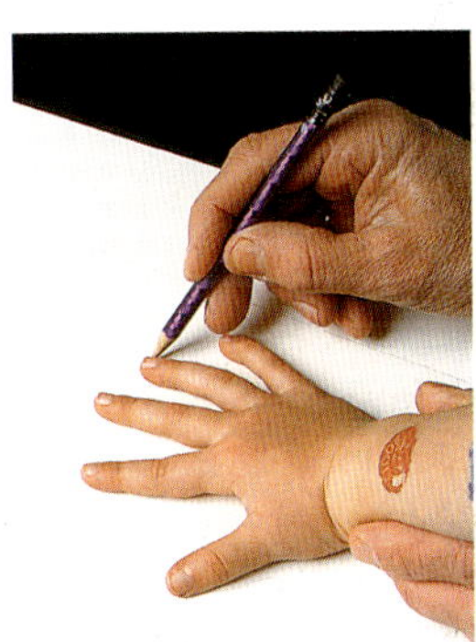

2 Draw around a shape that is smaller than the deckle within the rectangle already marked on the foamboard.

3 Use a craft knife over a cutting mat to cut out the shape you have drawn.

▶

Use an interestingly shaped, small object to emboss the top of a sheet. I have made a card shape using my daughter's hand and the resulting paper features an imprint that is a lasting memento.

LEFT *"Communication." Plaster molds were made from telephones and wet sheets were then laminated onto the molds.*

RIGHT *A handprint can be framed as a memento or used as personalized notepaper.*

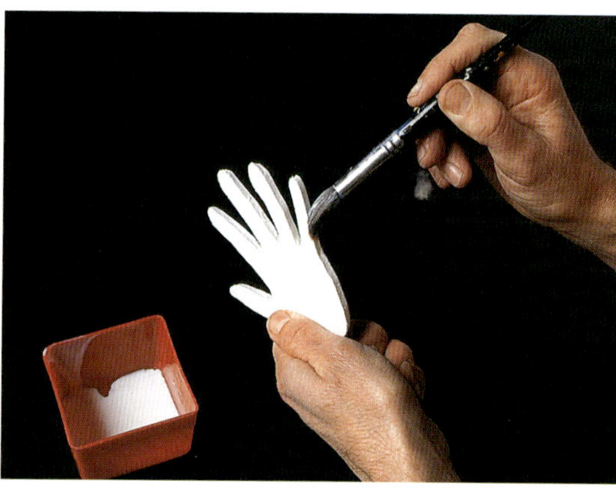

4 Waterproof the shape by applying a coat of acrylic varnish, especially around the outside edges of the shape. Leave to dry.

6 Lay several layers of felts on top of the shape, followed by a few blankets.

7 Assemble the press and proceed to press as usual (see page 39).

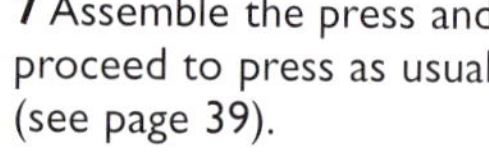

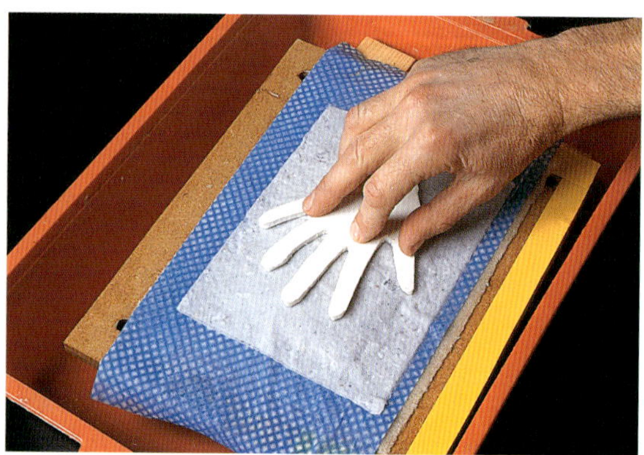

5 Form and couch a thick sheet of paper (see pages 28–30 and 36–37). Place the foamboard shape centrally on the sheet.

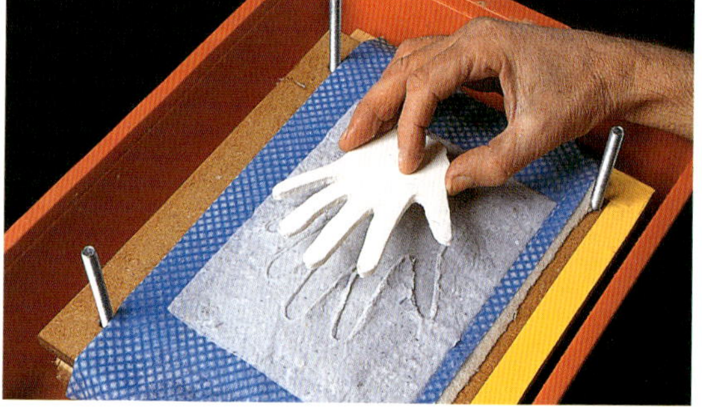

8 Disassemble the press and felt layers and carefully lift the shape off the sheet to reveal an impression left on the surface of the paper.

9 Hang the sheet up to dry (see page 40).

RIGHT *Electrical wire can be bent into any shape to create a unique embossed paper.*

When embossing using the press, only one sheet can be embossed at a time. A thicker layer of blankets is used to protect the objects being embossed, and remember not to apply too much pressure because the objects being embossed could go right through the paper. This danger is not apparent when embossing by hand, where the finished effect is slightly lighter than if you use a press.

RIGHT *This amazing effect was achieved by laminated cotton linters pulp being cast over a stone mill wheel and then left to dry for a month.*

Embossing with the press: using electrical wire

YOU WILL NEED

- **Electrical wire**
- **Long-nosed pliers**
- **Pulp in the vat (see pages 28–29), of a thick consistency**
- **Mold and deckle**
- **Press prepared for couching (see pages 36–37)**
- **Felts (disposable dishcloths)**
- **Several 10 x 8 in (25 x 20cm) blankets**
- **Clothes hanging line**
- **Clothes pegs**
- **Shallow tray**

1 Coil electrical wire around a pair of long-nosed pliers to make two concentric circles.

2 Form and couch a sheet of paper (see pages 28–30 and 36–37). Place the wire circles on the sheet of paper along with other lengths shaped with the pliers to create an interesting design.

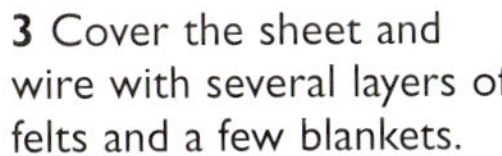

3 Cover the sheet and wire with several layers of felts and a few blankets.

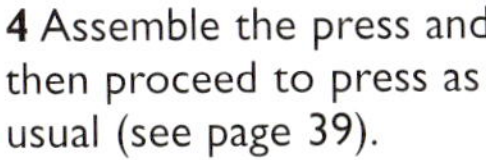

4 Assemble the press and then proceed to press as usual (see page 39).

5 Disassemble the press and felt layers and carefully lift the wire shapes off the sheet to reveal the impressions left on the surface of the paper.

6 Hang the sheet up to dry (see page 40).

Watermarks

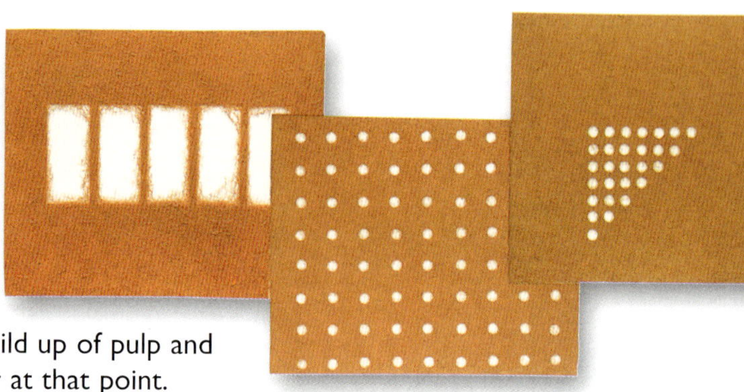

A watermark is basically an area of a sheet of paper that is thinner than the rest. This effect is achieved by placing an obstruction on the mesh of the mold that hinders the build up of pulp and so reduces the thickness of the paper at that point. When making a sheet with a watermark you need to use the mold without the deckle. Using sticky labels is the simplest method of

ABOVE *Creating watermarks on colored paper has a truly dramatic effect.*

Creating a watermark using sticky labels

YOU WILL NEED

- **Mold**
- **Sticky labels**
- **Pulp in the vat (see pages 28–29), of a thick consistency**
- **Press prepared for couching (see pages 36–37)**
- **Felts (disposable dishcloths)**
- **10 x 8 in (25 x 20cm) blanket**
- **Melamine sheet**
- **Paintbrush**
- **Roller**
- **Iron (optional)**
- **Flexible palette knife**

1 Lay the mold on a flat surface with the waterproof taped edges facing up. Stick labels onto the face of the mesh to create an interesting design.

3 Form a sheet without the deckle. The pulp is thinner over the area where the sticky labels are than elsewhere on the mold.

2 Turn the mold over so that the mesh is against a flat surface. Press down to ensure that the sticky labels have fully adhered to the mesh.

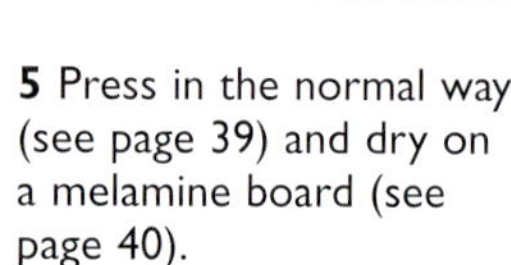

4 Couch a sheet (see pages 36–37). As you do so the labels remain on the mesh. You will be able to form another couple of sheets before they become too wet and need replacing. Build up a post (stack), if required.

5 Press in the normal way (see page 39) and dry on a melamine board (see page 40).

RIGHT *Wire stitching can create a delicate outline that offers a subtle watermark.*

making watermarks, but they will only stay on the mold for a limited period before falling off. The traditional method is to attach a wire pattern to the mesh. Once fixed to the mold you will be able to produce endless sheets of watermarked paper.

ABOVE *Even on white paper a watermark produces an attractive translucency.*

Creating a watermark using stitched wire

YOU WILL NEED

- Mold and deckle
- Paper
- Pencil
- Silver wire
- Pointed pliers
- File
- Needle and thread
- Pulp in the vat (see pages 28–29), of a thick consistency
- Press prepared for couching (see pages 36–37)
- Felts (disposable dishcloths)
- 10 x 8 in (25 x 20cm) blanket
- Melamine sheet
- Paintbrush
- Roller
- Iron (optional)
- Flexible palette knife

1 Draw around the inside of the deckle on a sheet of paper. Then draw the watermark motif, as a continuous line, inside the marked rectangle.

2 Use pointed pliers to manipulate a length of silver wire into the motif designed on the paper.

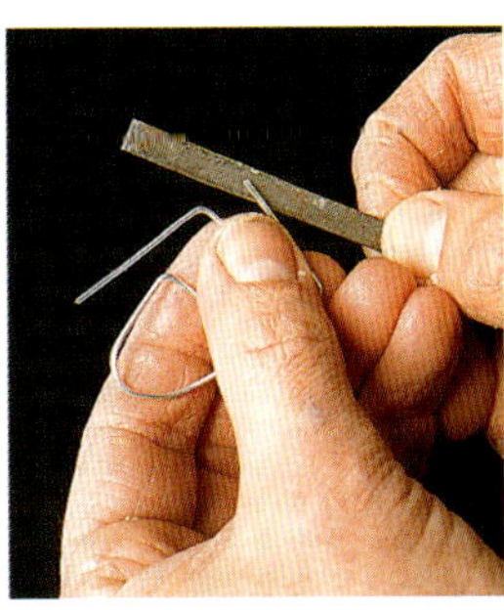

3 Cut the wire with the pliers then file each end of the silver wire motif to prevent a jagged edge catching in the fibers of the formed sheet.

4 Hold the wire motif against the mesh of the mold. Turn the mold upside down while still holding the wire, then sew the wire in place through the mesh.

5 Form a sheet without the deckle. The pulp is thinner over the wire motif than elsewhere on the mold.

6 Couch the sheet and build up a post (stack), if required (see pages 36–37).

7 Press in the normal way (see page 39) and dry on a melamine board (see page 40).

also see the following pages
Before you start: making a shaped deckle only 16 • **Making pulp from part-processed fibers** 22–23 • **Sheet forming: sheet forming with part-processed fiber pulp** 30 **and sheet forming with a shaped deckle** 35 **Couching** 36–37 • **Pressing** 39 **Drying** 40–41 • **Watermarks: creating a watermark using stitched wire** 63

Project 2

Stationery set

In this project a shaped deckle really comes into its own, making a shaped paper that, with minimal folding, can be made into an envelope.

The embedded addition of grated wax crayons to the pulp makes for an interesting and fun envelope, while the plain sheet of watermarked paper provides the perfect complement.

The star shape used to make the watermark is a child's toy, but any simple shape is suitable, as long as the wire can be wrapped around it in one continuous length. Since the paper and the envelope are likely to be written on, size must be added to the vat of pulp before forming the sheet.

YOU WILL NEED

- **Cutting mat**
- **Pen**
- **Steel ruler**
- **9¾ x 13¾ in (24.5 x 35cm) strip of ⅛ in (3mm) thick foamboard**
- **Set square**
- **Craft knife**
- **Acrylic varnish**
- **Paintbrush**
- **Cheese grater**
- **Wax crayons, red, blue, and yellow**
- **Plate**
- **Sized cotton linters pulp in the vat (see pages 22–23 and 28)**
- **Mold**
- **Sheet forming, couching, pressing, and drying equipment (see pages 28–41)**
- **Paper folder**
- **Glue stick**
- **Silver wire**
- **Star shape**
- **Pointed pliers**
- **Wire cutters**
- **Needle and thread**

1 Working on a cutting mat, draw a 1 in (2.5cm) wide margin along each side of the foamboard to form a 7¾ x 11¾ in (19.5 x 30cm) rectangle. Mark the center point of each side and draw lines from each center point to the center point on the adjacent side to form a diamond shape.

2 Mark the center point of each diagonal line and make another mark ⅜ in (1cm) either side of this center point. From the center point of a diagonal line, use a set square to draw a ¼ in (6mm) line at right angles to the diagonal. Draw a diagonal line from the top of this new line to the marks on either side of the center point. Repeat on all sides of the diamond in order to create notches.

3 Place the steel ruler along the drawn lines and use a craft knife to cut out the foamboard shaped deckle, as above. Waterproof the shaped deckle by painting on two coats of acrylic varnish and leaving to dry.

4 Using a cheese grater, grate some wax crayons to produce a mound of rainbow-colored specks of wax.

5 Add the grated wax to sized cotton linters pulp in the vat, and form a sheet with the shaped deckle held tightly against the mesh of the mold, remembering to hold it firmly in place as you lift it from the vat. Couch, press, and dry the sheet as usual.

6 When the paper is dry it can be folded into an envelope shape. Lay the sheet flat on your work surface, smooth side down in this case. Line the metal ruler up with the center point of two opposite notches and fold the flap over the ruler. Repeat this process to fold over the other flaps.

7 Using a paper folder, press down firmly on the crease and bring the folder along the crease toward you to score the fold.

8 Open out the flaps and apply a spot of glue to the point of one of the short opposite flaps and stick together. Apply a line of glue, about ½ in (1.5cm) in, along the edge of the bottom flap, fold it over, and stick down.

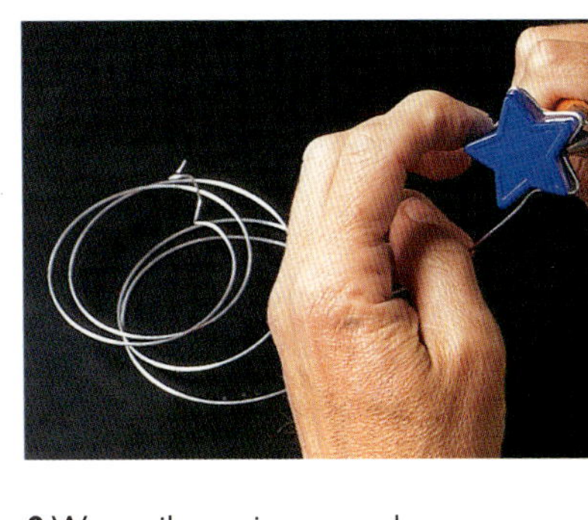

9 Wrap silver wire around a star shape and use pliers to press it into the shape. Continue all around the shape, finishing at the exact point where the wire began. Remove the formed wire from the shape and snip off the excess wire.

10 Position the wire centrally at the top of the mold and sew it to the mesh using a needle and thread.

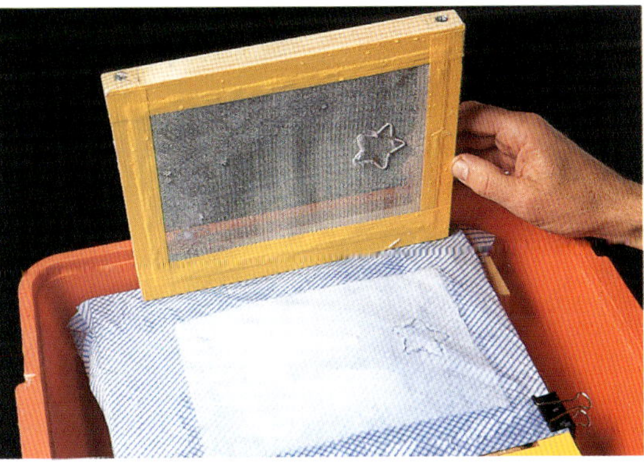

11 Form a sheet of cotton linters paper using the mold without a deckle: you can use sized cotton linters pulp with or without wax crayon shavings. Couch, press, and dry the sheet in the usual way.

Casting

Think of casting as akin to making a jelatin mold. The inside of the mold is the negative, and the jello makes a positive impression of it. Alternatively, a cast can be made directly from an object that produces a negative impression.

When casting, an important consideration is the amount of shrinkage of the pulp as it dries. The more a pulp shrinks, the more the paper will tend to distort and so produce a less faithful copy of the original from which you are making a cast.

Casting from a found object

YOU WILL NEED

- **Petroleum jelly**
- **Garden trowel**
- **2 lightly pressed sheets of cotton linters paper (see pages 22–23 and 28–39)**
- **Paintbrush**

BELOW *Once dry, the finished piece can be left in its natural state or decorated.*

ABOVE *Cotton linters paper was laminated and cast on an old stone sink.*

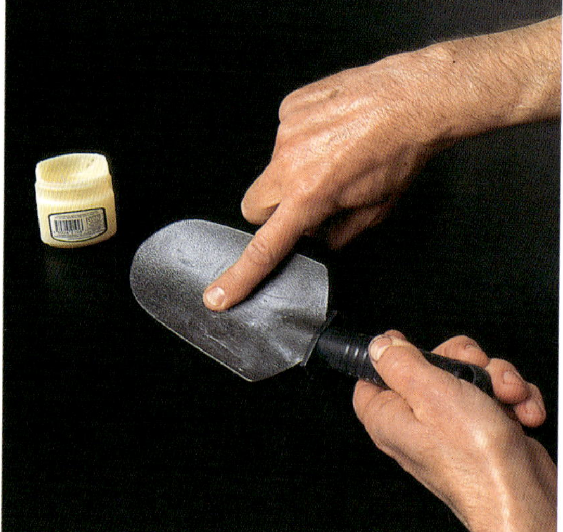

1 Rub petroleum jelly over the inside surface of a garden trowel so that it is thinly coated.

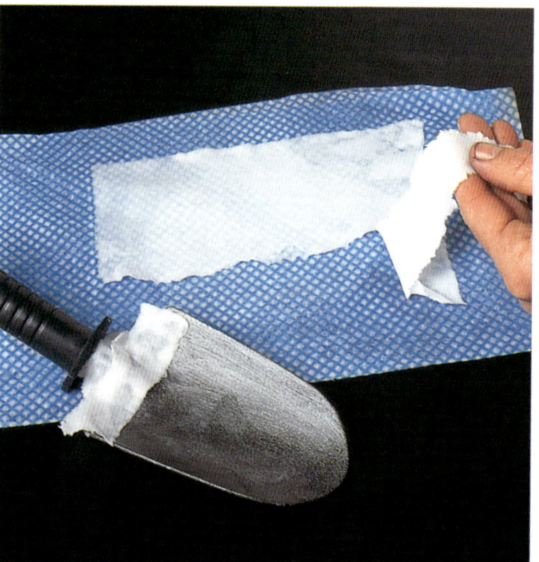

2 Tear off a roughly 1 in (2.5cm) strip lengthwise from a sheet of cotton linters paper. Tear a piece off this strip slightly wider than the trowel and lay it horizontally across the trowel, pressing down firmly. Tear off another strip from the sheet.

RIGHT *Entitled "Ishtar" by the artist, this piece was cast before assembling.*

For this reason it is best to use a short-fibered pulp such as cotton linters, where the amount of shrinkage is kept to a minimum. As a general rule, a long-fibered pulp will have a high rate of shrinkage while a short-fibered pulp will have a low rate of shrinkage. That is not to say that you cannot use a long-fibered pulp to cast. Once you have gained experience with these casting techniques it is worth casting with different types of pulp, such as plant and recycled paper, to learn to judge their suitability to produce casts.

Paper proves to be a very versatile and light material for casting, and there are several methods available. The first, sheet casting, uses a

3 Position more strips of paper horizontally across the trowel, ensuring the strip being laid overlaps the preceding one by 1/8 in (3mm). Continue until the whole surface is covered.

5 Carefully tear off the paper hanging over the edge of the trowel, and leave the cast to dry.

4 Lay longer strips lengthwise on top of those already laid. To ensure that these strips bond to those underneath, hold a paintbrush vertically and then use downward strokes to tap each strip into position.

6 Carefully lift the dry paper cast off the trowel.

lightly pressed sheet of formed paper torn into strips to produce a thin laminate. The strips are laid on the surface of the mold slightly overlapping one another. Another layer of strips is placed on top, at right angles to the one underneath. The cross-bonding of paper produces a very tough and light cast. The number of layers required depends on the size of the cast. Alternatively, a single sheet can be laid over a mold. In both cases, the paper used needs to be wet because it is the cellulose in the fibers that bonds the paper cast together once it has thoroughly dried. Another casting technique is pulp casting, in which pulp is pushed tightly into a mold and allowed to dry.

Casting from a plaster mold

YOU WILL NEED

- **Plaster**
- **Mixing bowl**
- **Shallow box**
- **Stones**
- **Petroleum jelly**
- **Lightly pressed sheet of cotton linters paper (see pages 22–23 and 28–39)**

2 Before the plaster has had a chance to set, arrange some stones in it. Wait for about an hour for the plaster to set and the mold is complete.

1 Mix some plaster, being sure to follow the manufacturer's instructions. Carefully pour the plaster into a shallow box, taking care not to overfill it. Gently tap the sides of the box to expel any trapped air.

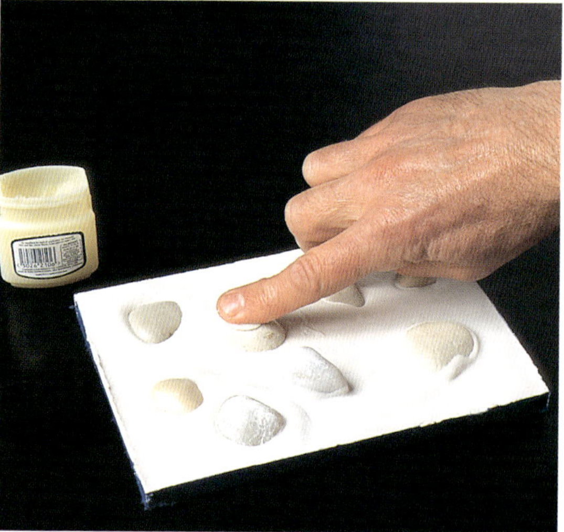

3 Apply a thin coat of petroleum jelly to the surface of the mold.

LEFT AND FAR LEFT *Cast on the same mold and then painted with watercolor, these pieces show that each casting is unique.*

ABOVE *The amazing flexibility of paper is demonstrated by the finished piece created in the technique below.*

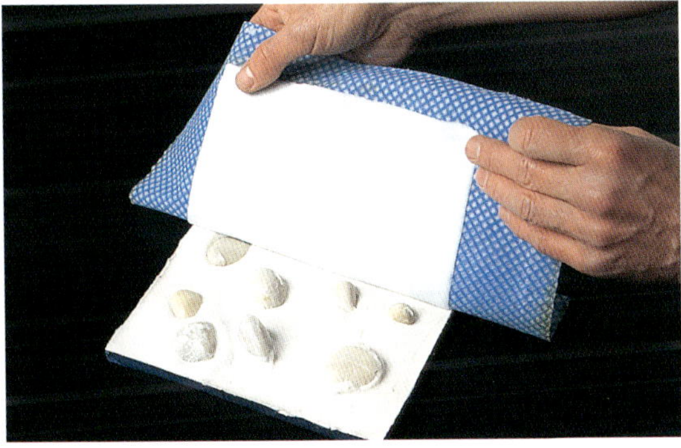

4 Take a lightly pressed cotton linters sheet still on its felt, and position the long edge of the sheet along the long edge of the mold. Let the felt and sheet slowly lie down on top of the mold.

6 Carefully lift off the felt and leave the cast to dry.

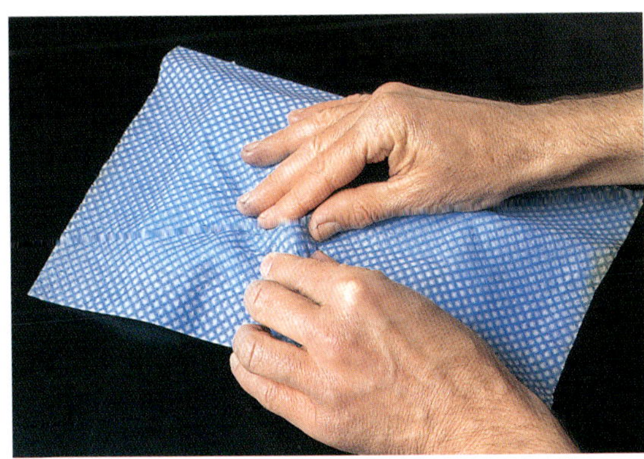

5 Gently press the felt and formed sheet around the projections and surface of the mold, taking special care not to tear the paper.

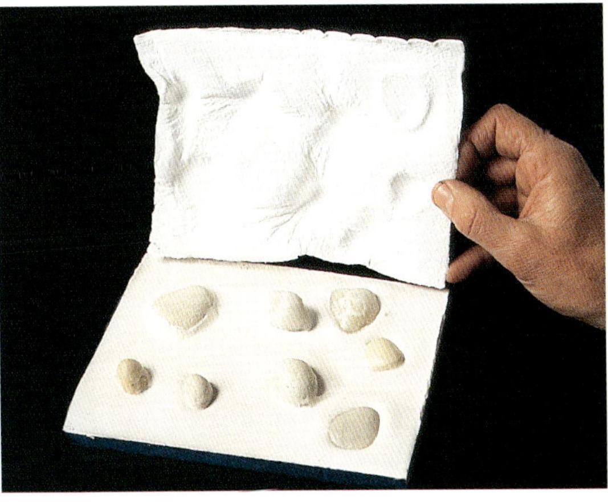

7 Carefully lift the cast paper off the mold, avoiding damaging the cast as it is lifted.

Paper shrinks as it dries, so it is preferable to take a cast on the inside surfaces of an object. If cast around the outside of an object the paper tears as it contracts when drying. You can make casts from found objects, by making your own molds, or using ready-made molds, and you can even combine the sheet and pulp casting techniques.

Casting from a clay mold

YOU WILL NEED

- **Wrench**
- **6 x 3 x 1 in (15 x 7.5 x 2.5cm) block of clay**
- **Petroleum jelly**
- **Cotton swab**
- **Lightly pressed sheet of cotton linters paper (see pages 22–23 and 28–39)**
- **Paintbrush**

BELOW *Casts can be made from found objects or ready-made molds.*

ABOVE *The rich colors combined with the undulations of the cast paper produces a work full of movement and depth.*

1 Press a wrench firmly into the surface of a clay block. On lifting it out you now have a mold containing a negative impression of the wrench.

2 Coat the entire surface of the mold with petroleum jelly, using a cotton swab to get into the awkward crevices of the mold.

When casting, petroleum jelly is used as a release agent. It forms a barrier between the surface of the mold and the cast and prevents the paper sticking to the mold, ensuring that the cast can be easily removed when dried. Blister packaging (molded plastic packaging) and ready-made molds, because they are plastic, do not need a release agent since the paper will not adhere to their shiny, non-absorbent surfaces. But if you are in any doubt it is better to play safe and apply petroleum jelly to the surface of your mold.

Casting from blister packaging

YOU WILL NEED

- **Esparta pulp (see pages 22–23)**
- **Plastic bowl**
- **Blister packaging**
- **Sponge**
- **Hair dryer**

1 Before adding pulp to the mold, gently squeeze a small handful to expel some of the water. The pulp still needs to be wet so don't squeeze it completely dry.

2 Place the pulp, a small amount at a time, into some blister packaging that forms the mold. Make sure the pulp is pushed down tightly.

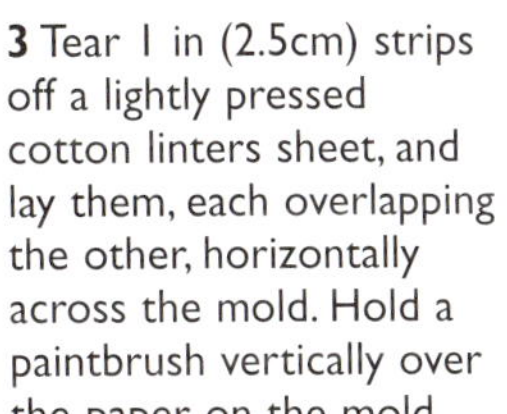

3 Tear 1 in (2.5cm) strips off a lightly pressed cotton linters sheet, and lay them, each overlapping the other, horizontally across the mold. Hold a paintbrush vertically over the paper on the mold and use a stippling action to push it into the deep recesses. Lay another series of overlapping strips lengthwise on top, tapping them down with the brush. Leave to dry.

4 Slowly and gently lift the cast paper away from the mold.

LEFT *Plastic blister packaging, used to protect a wide range of products, is easily found and provides an ideal mold for casting.*

When pulp is used to make a cast its drying time will depend not only on the surrounding temperature but also on the thickness of the cast—the thicker it is, the longer it will take to dry, and vice versa. Even though the surface of the cast may feel dry, it does not necessarily mean the pulp has dried all the way through, so give it plenty of time.

Remember that not all pulps dry at the same rate; if, when using a combination of pulps, one does dry more quickly, it will distort the cast as it shrinks. Unless you want

3 Use a sponge at intervals to soak up the excess water that collects on the surface of the cast.

4 Once the pulp is in the mold to a depth of ½ in (1.5cm), use a hair dryer to speed up the drying process. Hold it 9–12 in (23–30cm) from the cast and move it back and forth to ensure an even distribution of heat across the surface. Once dry, turn the blister pack over, and shake gently until the cast comes out.

Casting from ready-made molds

YOU WILL NEED

- **3 ready-made molds**
- **Esparta pulp (see pages 22–23)**
- **Kraft pulp (see pages 22–23)**
- **Cotton linters pulp (see pages 22–23)**
- **2 lightly pressed sheets of cotton linters paper (see pages 22–23 and 28–39)**
- **Paintbrush**

BELOW *recycled pulp was layered and impressed with natural objects.*

1 Fill one mold with kraft pulp and one with esparta pulp. Pack the pulps in tightly, then squeeze out some, not all, of the water. Repeat with cotton linters pulp in the third mold.

this to be a feature of the cast, test the drying times of the pulps beforehand. The three types of pulp I have used in the technique with the ready-made mold (see below) all dry at the same rate, thus preventing any distortion.

RIGHT *Three types of pulp were used in this mold: kraft, esparta, and cotton linters.*

2 Lay a lightly pressed sheet of cotton linters paper over the top of the complete mold.

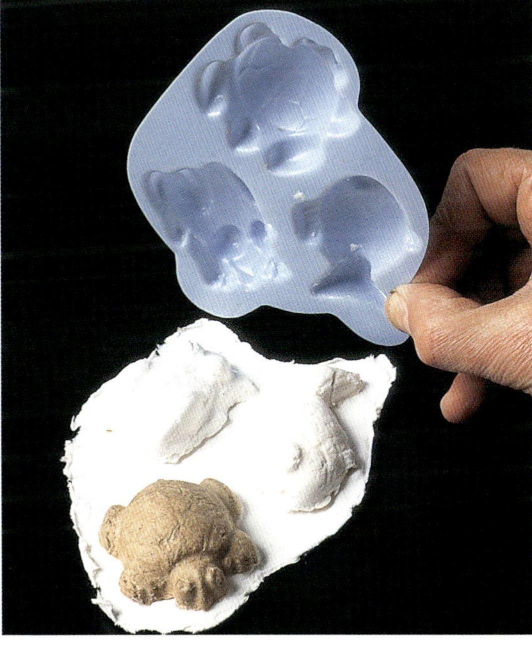

4 Turn the cast over and lift off the molds to reveal this interesting paper compilation.

3 To strengthen this backing sheet, add strips of cotton linters paper on top and press them down into place using a paintbrush held vertically over the sheet. Allow the cast to dry.

also see the following pages
Casting: casting from a clay mold 70
Making pulp from part-processed fibers 22–23 • **Sheet forming: sheet forming with part-processed fibers pulp** 30
Couching 36–37 • **Pressing** 39

Project 3

Still-life relief

This project shows how it is possible to be creative and resourceful in producing a lasting work of art. The result will be considerably enhanced if you paint the piece before framing it to hang in your home.

The main consideration with this project is the design of the mold. You need to have an idea of the composition of the cast, as the shape of the mold will be the negative of this—so, in a way, you need to start thinking backwards! For instance, here, we create a line of bottles sitting on a shelf. In the cast the shelf is sticking out, so in the mold it needs to be recessed. Likewise with the bottles: they are pushed into the clay to create a negative impression.

YOU WILL NEED

- **Rolling pin**
- **Modeling clay**
- **Steel ruler**
- **2 15 in (38cm) lengths of 1 x ¾ in (2.5 x 2cm) soft wood**
- **Flexible palette knife**
- **Petroleum jelly**
- **3 miniature glass bottles**
- **Glass spice jar**
- **8 lightly pressed sheets of cotton linters paper (see pages 22–23 and 28–39)**
- **Paintbrush**
- **Sponge**

1 Use a rolling pin to roll out a slab of modeling clay until it is a 10 x 7 in (25 x 18cm) rectangle about 1 in (2.5cm) thick. You will find it easier to maintain a consistent thickness by rolling out the clay between two lengths of 1 in (2.5cm) thick wood. Keep both ends of the rolling pin on the wood and roll back and forth until you have a smooth surface.

2 To establish a baseline for the relief, use a palette knife to mark a line in the clay 1½ in (4cm) up from the bottom edge, scoring along the edge of a steel ruler.

3 Rub petroleum jelly onto one half of each miniature glass bottle and the spice jar, to stop them sticking to the clay.

4 Petroleum jelly side down, lay the glass containers along the top of the clay slab to determine their positions, aligning the bases with the marked baseline. When you are happy with your arrangement, hold the first jar at a slight tilt above the clay and push the bottom along the baseline. Continue to lower the container down into the surface of the clay. Push it into the clay halfway, then carefully and gently ease it out again, bottom first, in a rocking motion, as above.

5 Repeat step 4 to impress all but the last container. Place one of the lengths of wood against the end of the clay slab before pressing in the final container. This will prevent any distortion to the edge of the clay slab.

6 Use the knife to cut away a slab of clay from the baseline down, deep enough to go beyond the base of each of the bottles. This is for the shelf. Slice along horizontally and peel the clay away.

7 Coat the surface of the mold with petroleum jelly, covering it entirely and going into the impressions where you can.

8 Tear lightly pressed cotton linters sheets into strips and lay them, each overlapping the other, horizontally across the mold. Hold a paintbrush vertically over the paper on the mold and use a stippling action to push it into the deep recesses. Lay another series of overlapping strips lengthwise on top, tapping them down with the paintbrush.

9 Lay down a final layer of paper strips, at right angles to the second layer, and press down as usual. Use a sponge to compress the strips together and soak up any excess water lying on the surface. Leave in a warm place to dry, then carefully lift the cast paper away from the mold.

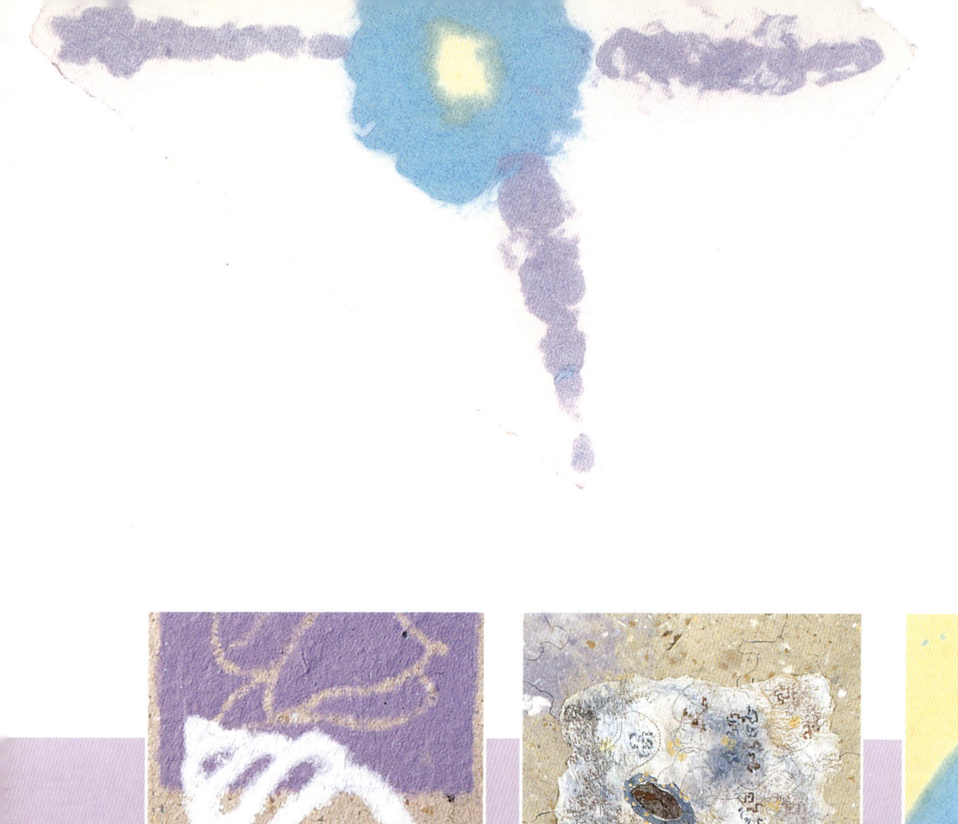

using color

Color adds an exciting dimension to your papermaking skills, from discovering the different methods of creating colored sheets to painting with colored pulps. There is huge scope for experimentation and a myriad of ways in which to dye paper pulp. Begin with these simple techniques and soon you will have the confidence to follow your own ideas.

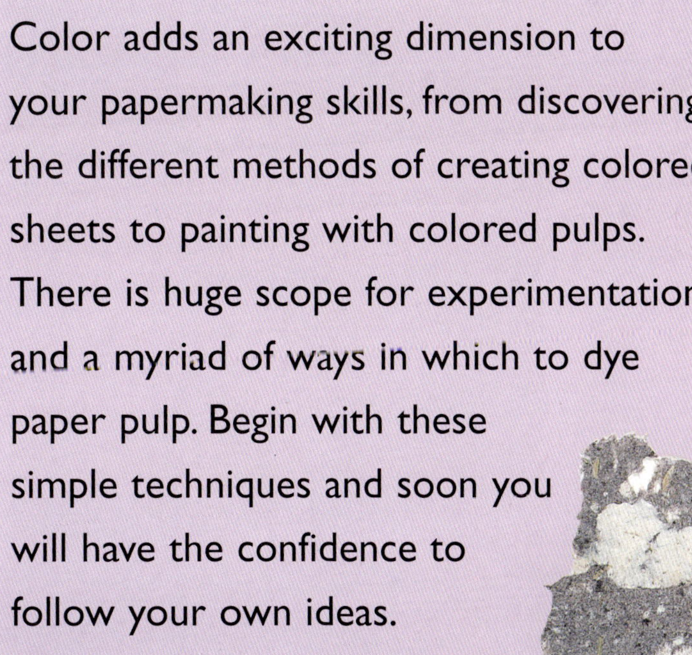

Dyeing pulps

There are a number of techniques you can use to determine the final color of the paper you make. When using plant fibers to make paper, the plant material used dictates the color of the paper. However, you may want to keep the textural qualities of a plant paper but use it for something other than decorative purposes, such as painting or writing on, in which case you can bleach the plant fibers to produce a lighter colored pulp for sheet forming.

ABOVE *Handmade paper made with dyed pulps, ripped into strips and then machine stitched together.*

Bleaching plant fiber pulp

YOU WILL NEED

- **Protective gloves**
- **Household bleach**
- **Measuring jug**
- **Plastic bucket**
- **Plant fiber pulp (see pages 24–25)**
- **Wooden implement for stirring**
- **Strainer**
- **Net curtain fabric**
- **Sheet forming, couching, pressing, and drying equipment (see pages 28–41)**

1 Wearing protective gloves, measure out ½ pint (300ml) of bleach and add this to 4 pints (2.4l) of cold water in a plastic bucket.

2 Add enough plant fiber pulp to the diluted bleach to enable it to float around freely. Stir well and leave for 4 hours.

RIGHT *Recycled paper pulps were enhanced with pigments and onion-skin fibers to produce the variety of colors shown here.*

In a similar way, the original color of the paper used to make recycled paper pulp will affect the color of the final sheet. The techniques I describe in this section are ostensibly for use on recycled and part-processed pulp such as the cotton linters I use here. You could use a synthetic dye to create paper with the texture of plant fiber combined with a very bright color to produce a combination of the natural and the manufactured.

Alternatively, you may feel it is more appropriate to use a natural dye and retain a completely organic look to the final paper.

3 Empty the bucket into a strainer lined with net curtain fabric to collect the bleached plant fiber pulp. Thoroughly rinse in cold water.

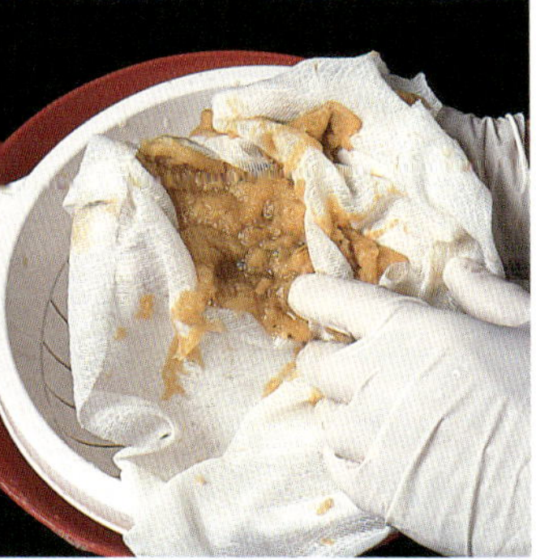

4 The plant fiber pulp is now a lot lighter in color. Form, couch, press, and dry a sheet as normal (see pages 28–39).

Coloring recycled paper pulp with more paper

YOU WILL NEED

- **2 pint (1.2l) food blender**
- **Red crepe paper**
- **Scissors**
- **Glass bowl**
- **Recycled paper pulp (see pages 20–21)**
- **Spoon**
- **Sheet forming, couching, pressing, and drying equipment (see pages 28–41)**

1 Fill a blender jug half full with water. Cut up some red crepe paper into thin strips and add enough to the blender to allow the pieces to float freely.

2 Operate the blender in short 30-second bursts until the paper has been completely broken down. If the blender labors too much, switch it off (unplug it as well) and take out some of the pulp, then add more water and start again. Tip the pulp into a glass bowl.

▶

LEFT The artist used different colored recycled papers to achieve the pulp colors seen here.

It is also possible to add specialist paper dye to a pulp, although cold water fabric dyes are just as effective. Although both types of dye come in a variety of vibrant colors, once you have mastered using the basic hues it is worth experimenting with mixing them to see what interesting combinations you can achieve. Once pulp has been colored it can be stored for later use in the same way as described earlier in the book (see pages 21 and 27).

Using fabric dyes

YOU WILL NEED

- **Protective gloves**
- **Cold water fabric dye**
- **Measuring jug**
- **Spoon**
- **2 glass bowls**
- **Cotton linters pulp (see pages 22–23)**
- **Strainer**
- **Net curtain fabric**
- **Sheet forming, couching, pressing, and drying equipment (see pages 28–41)**

1 Wearing protective gloves and following the manufacturer's instructions, mix concentrated fabric dye powder with the specified quantity of cold water and stir well.

2 Half fill a glass bowl with cotton linters pulp and add enough dye to cover the pulp and allow it to be moved around freely in the dye. Stir the dye well into the pulp. Leave the mixture to stand overnight.

BELOW The finished piece of paper will dry to a lighter color than the pulp.

3 Add approximately half as much recycled paper pulp to the red pulp and mix the two together.

4 Form, couch, press, and dry the sheet as normal (see pages 28–41). The sheet of recycled paper is delicately colored.

If you have an aversion to manufactured dyes, then natural dyes are a viable alternative. One approach would be to forage for interestingly colored plants and vegetables and extract the dye from them, though, because of its seasonal nature, this is a long-term project. In the short term, there are other solutions, such as frozen berries or fresh vegetables from the grocer or supermarket. Or experiment with the various foodstuffs in the kitchen cupboard, such as coffee, tea, food colors, or turmeric.

ABOVE *Stunning colors have been achieved by coloring cotton linters pulp with fiber-reactive dyes.*

3 Tip the dyed pulp and excess dye into a strainer lined with net curtain fabric over another bowl to collect the excess dye for later use. Rinse the pulp in cold water and squeeze it out in the fabric.

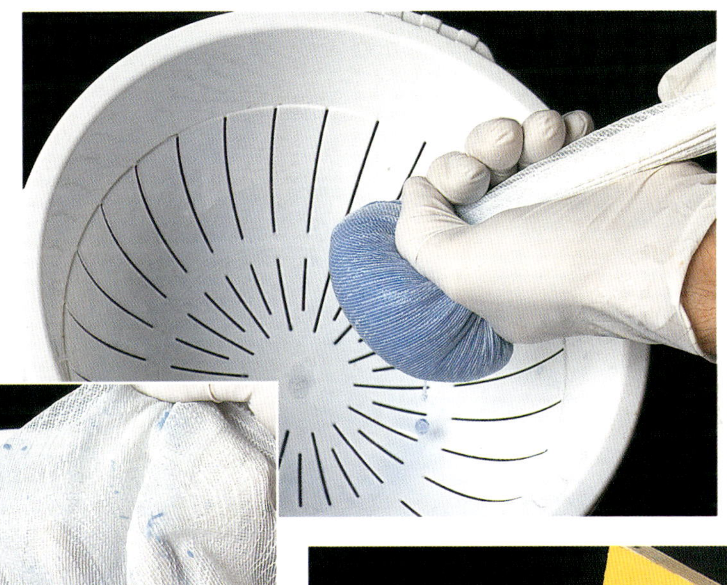

4 Once you have released the last remaining liquid you can either store the dyed pulp in a glass jar for use at a later date, or proceed to make colored paper now.

5 Form, couch, press, and dry the sheet as normal (see pages 28–41), remembering to wear gloves when handling the dyed pulp.

Remember always to make sure you adequately protect yourself and your work area when preparing or using dyes, since they can be permanent. Any unused dyes, whether natural or chemical, can be stored in glass jars and used at a later date, so you do not need to worry about making too much dye. It is very important that after you have dyed the pulp it is rinsed properly to rid the pulp of the last vestiges of dye. Although this greatly minimizes the risk of color running when using fabric or specialist paper dyes, you should be aware that if you are using natural material or

Using natural dyes: frozen berries

YOU WILL NEED

- **A handful of frozen berries**
- **2 pint (1.2l) food blender**
- **Sieve**
- **Plastic bowl**
- **Wooden spoon**
- **Cotton linters pulp (see pages 22–23)**
- **Strainer**
- **Net curtain fabric**
- **Glass bowl**
- **Spoon**
- **Protective gloves**
- **Sheet forming, couching, pressing, and drying equipment (see pages 28–41)**

1 Defrost the frozen berries and empty them into a blender jug. Blend until they have been reduced to a purée.

2 Hold a sieve over a plastic bowl and tip the puréed berries into the sieve, allowing the dye to drain through to the bowl beneath.

3 Use a wooden spoon to squeeze the last drops of dye out from the berries. Put the berries in the sieve to one side; you may want to use them later.

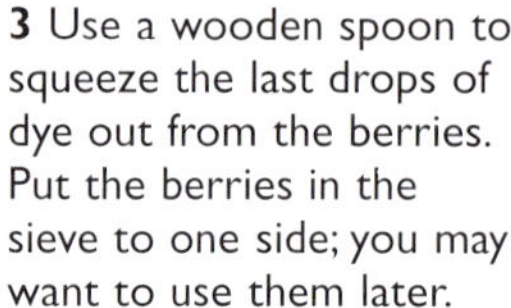

4 Half fill a glass bowl with cotton linters pulp and add the dye.

5 Stir the dye into the pulp and leave overnight to allow the dye to saturate the fibers of the pulp. Then tip the dyed pulp into a strainer lined with net curtain fabric over another bowl to collect the excess dye. Rinse the dyed pulp in cold water, and squeeze it out in the fabric to release the liquid.

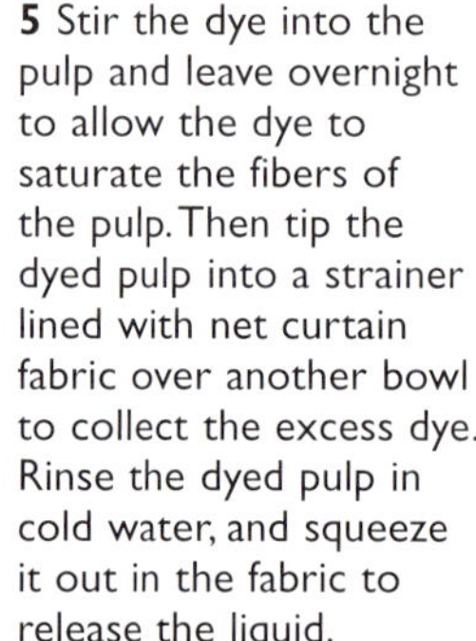

LEFT *Frozen berries produce an unexpectedly subtle color with interesting speckles.*

LEFT Acrylic paint was used to color recycled papers, which were formed without mold or deckle.

foodstuffs dyes there may be a tendency for the color to run, especially when using a combination of colored pulps together. It is advisable to check beforehand the colorfastness of the pulps you intend to use. You may find that the colors from the pulps will bleed into one another. It is up to you whether to take advantage of this as it is possible to get some very interesting coloring effects in this way, especially when using a pulp painting or casting technique.

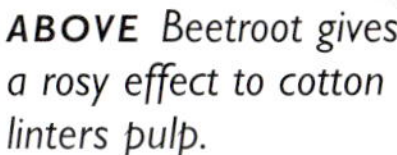

ABOVE Beetroot gives a rosy effect to cotton linters pulp.

6 Form, couch, press, and dry the sheet as normal (see pages 28–41), remembering to wear gloves when handling the dyed pulp.

7 Alternatively, add the dregs in the sieve to the vat before you form a sheet of paper, to produce a sheet with an interesting coarse texture.

Using natural dyes: cooked vegetables

YOU WILL NEED

- **Cooked beetroot**
- **Knife**
- **Cutting board**
- **2 pint (1.2l) food blender**
- **Sieve**
- **Plastic bowl**
- **Wooden spoon**
- **Cotton linters pulp (see pages 22–23)**
- **Strainer**
- **Net curtain fabric**
- **Glass bowl**
- **Spoon**
- **Protective gloves**
- **Sheet forming, couching, pressing, and drying equipment (see pages 28–41)**

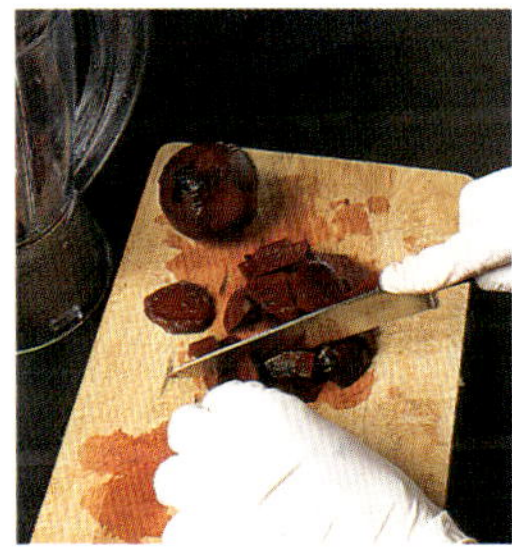

1 Cut some cooked beetroot into small chunks and add to a blender jug half full with water. Blend until the beetroot is reduced to a purée.

2 Follow steps 2–5 of Using Natural Dyes: Frozen Berries (see page 82) to dye some cotton linters pulp. Form, couch, press, and dry the sheet as normal (see pages 28–41), remembering to wear gloves when handling dyed pulp.

However, there will be times when this is not the effect required, and then you will need to use a fixative to ensure that the pulp is colorfast. To do this you can use a proprietary brand of dye fixative, or an adequate alternative would be to use salt, especially if using vegetable or foodstuffs as dyes.

An alternative method of dyeing a pulp, whether you are using fabric or natural dyes, is to add the dye during the beating

LEFT *In this work entitled "Sea," the artist has used specialized dyes and coffee grounds to color recycled and cotton linters paper.*

Using tea

YOU WILL NEED

- **6 tea bags**
- **Measuring jug**
- **Spoon**
- **Cotton linters pulp (see pages 22–23)**
- **Strainer**
- **Net curtain fabric**
- **Glass bowl**
- **Vat, any large plastic container**
- **Tea leaves**
- **Sheet forming, couching, pressing, and drying equipment (see pages 28–41)**

1 To get a really strong brew of tea, pour 1 pint (600ml) of boiling water over six tea bags in a measuring jug and leave to stew for a week. Before removing them from the jug, give each tea bag a final squeeze with a spoon.

2 Half fill a glass bowl with cotton linters pulp and add enough tea to cover the pulp and allow it to be stirred freely in the dye. Stir well and leave overnight to allow the fibers to absorb the color. Use the strainer lined with net curtain fabric to squeeze out excess liquid, then rinse the dyed pulp in cold water and squeeze it out in the fabric to release the remaining liquid.

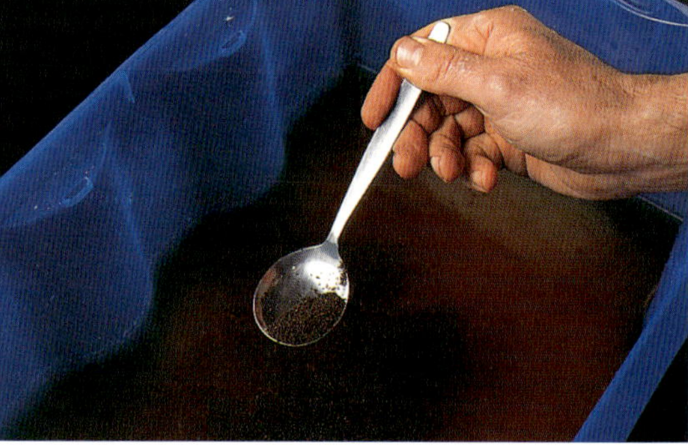

3 Half fill a vat with warm water and add the dyed pulp. Sprinkle a couple of spoonfuls of tea leaves evenly over the surface of the pulp in the vat.

4 Form, couch, press, and dry the sheet as normal (see pages 28–41). The tea will have colored the sheet and the tea leaves will have added that little bit of extra interest and individuality to the sheet.

process, instead of using water in the blender. The only difference in the procedure is that you must remember to collect the excess dye after you pour the pulp from the blender into a net-lined strainer. Using this method means the dye has a shorter contact time with the pulp, but the beating process allows a closer contact with the fibers sufficient for the pulp fibers to be dyed.

LEFT *Tea gives an aged effect to paper.*

Using turmeric

YOU WILL NEED

- Turmeric
- Measuring jug
- Teaspoon
- Glass bowl
- Cotton linters pulp (see pages 22–23)
- Strainer
- Net curtain fabric
- Sheet forming, couching, pressing, and drying equipment (see pages 28–41)

1 Add 2 tsp (10ml) of turmeric to 1 pint (600ml) of water in a measuring jug and stir well.

2 Half fill a glass bowl with cotton linters pulp and pour in the turmeric and water mix. Stir well and leave overnight to allow the fibers to absorb the color.

3 Tip the dyed pulp into a net-lined strainer and allow the excess liquid to strain away. Rinse and squeeze out the excess.

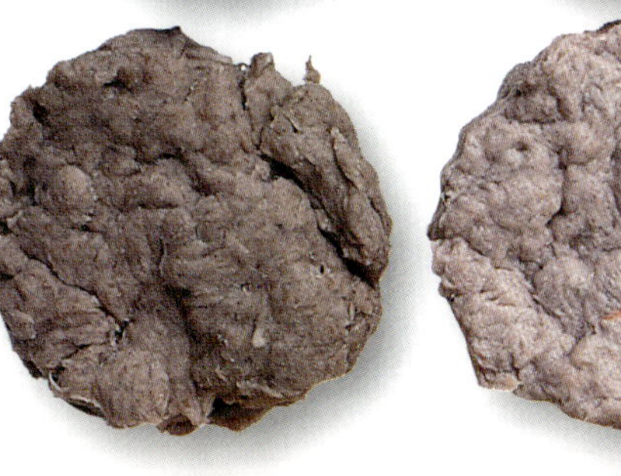

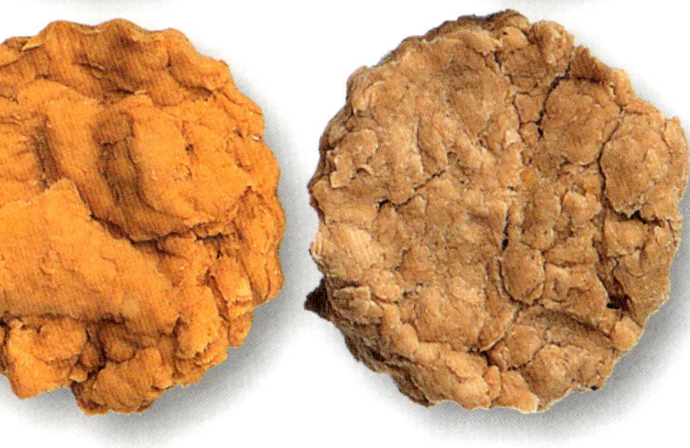

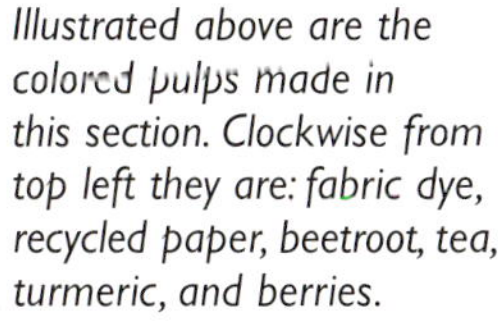

Illustrated above are the colored pulps made in this section. Clockwise from top left they are: fabric dye, recycled paper, beetroot, tea, turmeric, and berries.

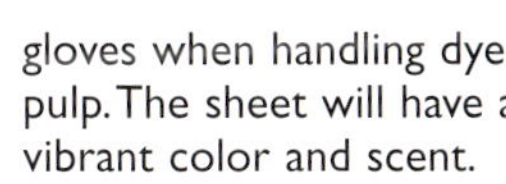

4 Form, couch, press, and dry the sheet as normal (see pages 28–41), remembering to wear gloves when handling dyed pulp. The sheet will have a vibrant color and scent.

Pulp painting

The use of color greatly increases your repertoire of papermaking possibilities. Pulp painting, literally painting with paper, uses colored pulps to produce a variety of interesting effects. You can pulp paint with the help of a stencil, either a ready-made shape or a motif you have designed yourself, or try freehand painting to be truly expressive.

The basic pulp-painting tool is a turkey baster, although plastic squeezy bottles are a suitable alternative. Applying the pulp with the

***ABOVE** The artist used pigments and bracken pulp with recycled paper to achieve the colors on this piece.*

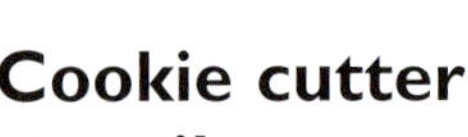

Cookie cutter stencils

YOU WILL NEED

- **Dilute dyed cotton linters pulps, blue, purple, and yellow (see pages 22–23 and 78–85)**
- **Formed sheet on the mold (see pages 28–29)**
- **Shallow tray**
- **2 lengths of 2 x 2 in (5 x 5cm) wood, to fit in the shallow tray**
- **Cookie cutters**
- **Turkey baster**
- **Couching, pressing, and drying equipment (see pages 36–41)**

1 It is important to note that the pulp you use needs to be quite dilute so that it can be sucked up into the turkey baster without getting stuck. Test the concentration of your pulp with the baster before you start. You should soon discover the correct ratio of pulp to water.

2 Place the mold with the formed sheet on two lengths of wood in a shallow tray. Position cookie cutters equidistant from one another on the formed sheet. Take care not to press the cutters down too firmly; they just need to rest on the surface of the paper.

RIGHT An attractive, delicate effect has been produced by the simple use of cookie cutters as stencils.

turkey baster will take some practice. Do not squeeze the pulp out too quickly as there is a danger that you will blow away not only the pulp you have already applied but also the formed sheet onto which you are painting. I would suggest that you spend some time mastering this technique on a piece of dry, scrap paper first. Once you have become proficient at this technique there is nothing to stop you giving full range to your imagination and producing some wonderful pieces of pulp painting.

3 Draw up some dilute dyed cotton linters pulp in the turkey baster. Position the baster over one cookie cutter and gently squeeze it to allow the pulp to come out. As you squeeze, move the baster along the inside edge of the shape, then fill in the center of the shape. Repeat with the other colors of dyed pulp in the other cookie cutters.

5 Couch the sheet as usual (see pages 36–37). What you see, above, is the underside of the sheet with the colored shapes showing through.

4 One at a time, carefully lift off the cutters from the formed sheet.

6 Lightly press the sheet (see page 39) and dry on a melamine board (see page 40).

RIGHT *Recycled pulp was painted and laminated to produce this multi-colored piece.*

When pulp painting you will find it easier to use a pulp with a short fiber such as cotton linters. Once diluted, the short fibers of the pulp are easily sucked into the turkey baster. If you are using a pulp with a longer fiber, such as plant, you will find it easier to use a spoon to apply the pulp to the painting.

All of the techniques I describe in this section use an already formed sheet on the mold as the basis of the painting. This is the simplest method to begin learning the pulp-painting technique. It allows you to develop your

Making your own stencil

YOU WILL NEED

- **Thin card**
- **Scissors**
- **Mold and deckle**
- **Shallow tray**
- **2 stones**
- **Spoon**
- **Dyed cotton linters pulps, red, purple, blue, and yellow (see pages 22–23 and 78–85)**
- **Couching, pressing, and drying equipment (see pages 36–41)**

1 Cut strips of card 1 in (2.5cm) wide. Place the mold on top of the deckle. Take a strip of card 10 in (25cm) long and position one end in a corner of the mold and the other in the diagonally opposite corner, to create an arc. Bend another strip at right angles 4½ in (11.5cm) from one end. Cut the strip 4½ in (11.5cm) from the right angle.

2 Cut a 4½ in (11.5cm) length of card and use it to join the other two 4½ in (11.5cm) lengths to create a triangle. Put a small amount of water into a shallow tray, no higher than the depth of the frame of the mold, and place the mold and deckle in the tray. Place a stone on opposite corners of the mold to act as weights and to keep the mold and deckle in place.

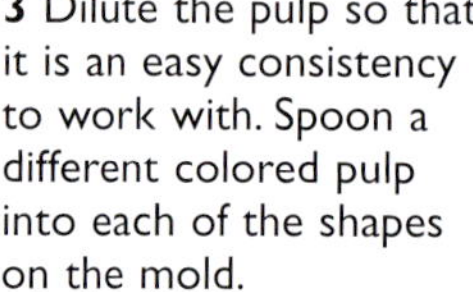

3 Dilute the pulp so that it is an easy consistency to work with. Spoon a different colored pulp into each of the shapes on the mold.

compositional skills by working within the boundary of the sheet of paper, much as you would when drawing or painting on dry paper. The difference, of course, is that the colored design or image that you produce also becomes part of the structural fabric of the paper.

RIGHT *The different colored pulps bond together in the pressing process.*

4 Use the handle end of the spoon to push the pulp tightly into the extremities of each shape.

5 Lift the mold and deckle from the water and rest them on the side of the tray, allowing the water to drain off. Carefully lift out each of the card strips. If there are any gaps between the colors, gently use the end of the spoon to push these areas of pulp together.

6 Swiftly couch the sheet (see pages 36–37). Don't worry, it will not fall apart. Press the sheet as usual (see page 39).

7 Lift the sheet off the couching mound on its felt and lay it on a melamine board to dry (see page 40). The pressing will have enabled the segments of the sheet to bond together.

ABOVE *Freehand pulp painting produces soft edges between the different colors.*

Once you have perfected pulp painting onto a formed sheet you should try painting directly onto the surface of the mold. This is slightly more difficult because you do not have a white base sheet to provide a backdrop for your composition, making it slightly more difficult to see what you are doing. To make a pulp painting in this way, position the mold without the deckle over a shallow tray and apply pulp directly onto the surface of the mold with a spoon or a turkey baster. After you have finished the painting, let as much water as possible drain off the mold, then rest it diagonally against a wall to dry. It can be left indoors or out, but if the former, make sure you lay newspaper or polythene on the floor to protect it from drips. Working in this way you will

Freehand pulp painting

YOU WILL NEED

- **Formed sheet of cotton linters pulp on the mold (see pages 30–31)**
- **2 lengths of 2 x 2 in (5 x 5cm) wood, to fit in the shallow tray**
- **Shallow tray**
- **Dyed cotton linters pulps, blue and yellow (see pages 22–23 and 78–85)**
- **Dilute dyed cotton linters pulp, purple (see pages 22–23 and 78–85)**
- **Spoon**
- **Turkey baster**
- **Couching, pressing, and drying equipment (see pages 36–41)**

1 Place the mold with the formed sheet on two lengths of wood in a shallow tray. Form a mound of blue cotton linters pulp in the center of the formed sheet with a spoon and make a cavity in the center. Use the spoon to fill the cavity with yellow pulp.

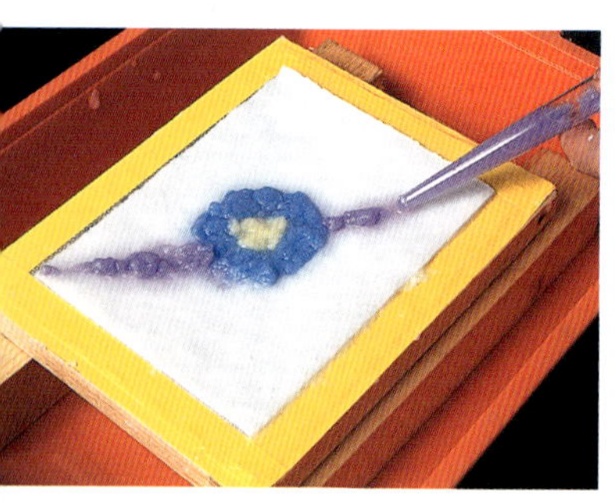

2 The dyed cotton linters pulp you use with the turkey baster needs to be quite dilute so that it can be sucked up into the baster without getting stuck. Be sure to test the concentration of your pulp with the baster before you start; after a while you will arrive at the correct ratio of pulp to water. Load the turkey baster with dilute purple pulp and create a line of pulp running diagonally from corner to corner.

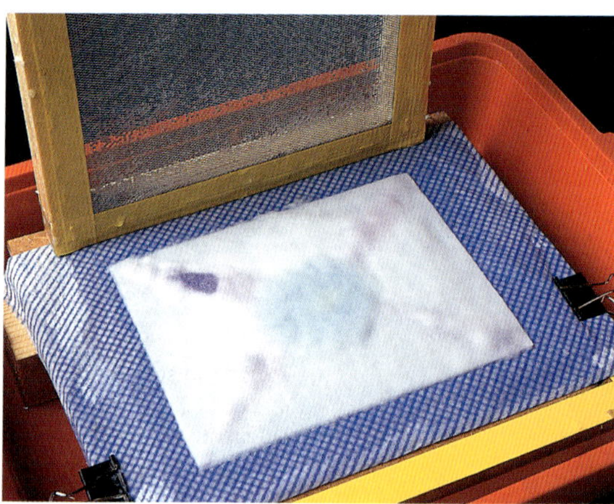

3 Couch the sheet before pressing it lightly (see page 39).

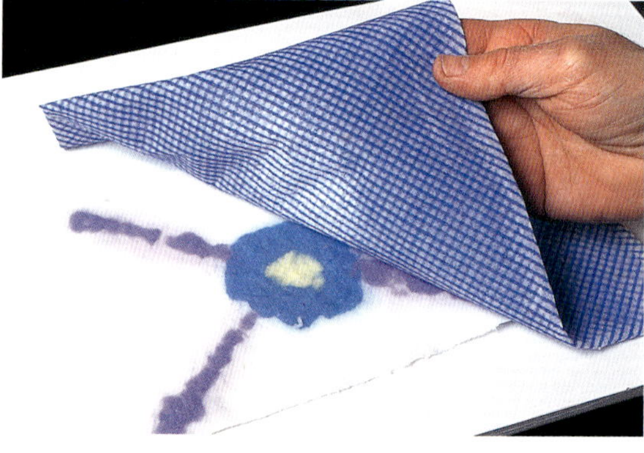

4 Remove the sheet from the press on its felt and lay it down on a melamine sheet to dry (see page 40).

need to leave the pulp painting on the mold to dry. This means that you will need a good supply of molds because they will be out of use while you wait for the pulp painting to dry.

RIGHT The artist dipped the mold in a pink pulp before adding painted and stitched paper in the center.

RIGHT The berry-dyed pulp and turmeric-dyed pulp fuse beautifully.

Infilling

YOU WILL NEED

- **Formed sheet of cotton linters pulp on the mold (see pages 30–31)**
- **2 lengths of 2 x 2 in (5 x 5cm) wood, to fit in the shallow tray**
- **Shallow tray**
- **Spoon**
- **Dyed cotton linters pulps, red, blue, and purple (see pages 22–23 and 78–85)**
- **Couching, pressing, and drying equipment (see pages 36–41)**

1 Position the mold with the formed sheet on two lengths of wood in a shallow tray. Use a spoon to carefully scrape away an area of the formed sheet without scraping away the edges of the sheet. Scrape away two smaller areas.

2 Use the spoon to fill each of these areas with different colored pulps that have been diluted to a malleable consistency. Use the spoon to tap the pulp onto the surface of the mold and up to the surrounding edges of the formed sheet.

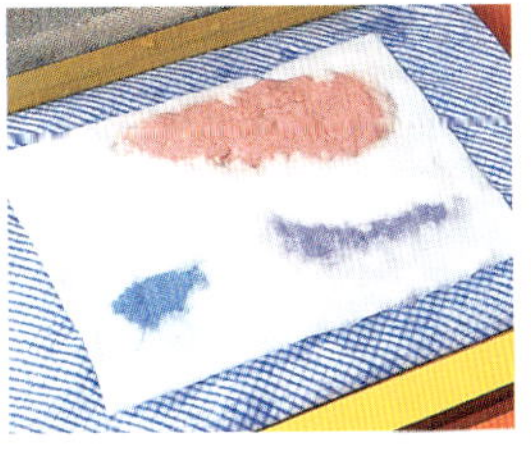

3 Couch the sheet as normal (see pages 36–37). From the underside you will be able to see the colored areas through the sheet. Press lightly (see page 39) and dry on a melamine surface (see page 40).

Dipping

YOU WILL NEED

- **Mold**
- **Berry-dyed cotton linters pulp (see page 82) in a vat (see pages 28–29)**
- **Turmeric-dyed cotton linters pulp (see page 85) in a vat (see pages 28–29)**
- **Couched cotton linters pulp sheet on the couching mound (see pages 22–23 and 36–37)**
- **Couching, pressing, and drying equipment (see pages 36–41)**

1 Hold the mold diagonally and, in one continuous movement, dip it halfway into a vat of berry pulp. As you lift it out, quickly bring it to a horizontal position.

2 Turn the mold around and dip the other half into turmeric pulp in a vat, diagonally as before, then bring it out in a horizontal position.

3 Couch this sheet on top of an already formed sheet on the couching mound (see pages 36–37). Press (see page 39) and dry on a melamine board (see page 40). The sheets will bond together.

also see the following pages
Pulp painting: making your own stencil 88
Making pulp from part-processed fibers 22–23 • **Dyeing pulps: using fabric dyes** 80
Sheet forming: sheet forming with part-processed fiber pulp 30
Couching 36–37 • **Pressing** 39
Drying 40–41

Project 4

Underwater scene

This project shows you how to combine the use of a stencil and freehand pulp-painting techniques. The composition uses fabric dyes to replicate a tropical underwater scene. Of course you could use other types of dye such as natural plant dyes to produce a landscape pulp painting.

Stencils give you control over the final composition. They are useful where a freehand technique would not produce such clarity. Don't worry about your drawing skills when making the stencil. Cut out an image from a magazine and draw around it onto the foamboard, or use a cookie cutter, which are made in a vast array of shapes. Whatever you choose, once you have mastered the technique you will be able to design and make ever more complex pulp paintings.

YOU WILL NEED

- **Pen**
- **5 x 8 in (13 x 20cm) strip of ⅛ in (3mm) thick foamboard**
- **Cutting mat**
- **Craft knife**
- **Acrylic varnish**
- **Paintbrush**
- **Formed sheet of blue cotton linters paper on mold (see pages 28 and 78–85)**
- **Shallow tray**
- **2 lengths of 2 x 2 in (5 x 5cm) wood, to fit in the shallow tray**
- **Dilute dyed cotton linters pulps, here yellow and green (see pages 22–23 and 78–85)**
- **Spoon**
- **Turkey baster**
- **Couching, pressing, and drying equipment (see pages 36–41)**

1 Draw a simple fish shape onto a 5 x 8 in (13 x 20cm) strip of ⅛ in (3mm) thick foamboard, using up as much of the foamboard as possible. Over a cutting mat, use a craft knife to cut out the stencil. Waterproof the stencil by applying two coats of acrylic varnish. Leave to dry.

2 Place a formed sheet of blue cotton linters paper on the mold on two lengths of wood in a shallow tray. Position the stencil in the bottom left-hand corner so that its sides line up with the sides of the formed sheet. Spoon diluted yellow cotton linters pulp into the stencil.

3 Use the end of the spoon to press down the yellow pulp firmly but carefully, to pack it down. Pay particular attention to the edges and push the pulp up against the sides of the stencil.

6 Draw up some dilute green cotton linters pulp in a turkey baster. Starting from the top, expel the pulp onto the blue sheet and move down in a linear fashion to create a seaweed effect.

4 Vertically lift off the stencil to reveal the fish shape. Reposition the stencil in the top right-hand corner of the sheet, lining the top edge of the stencil along the top edge of the sheet, but so that only half the stencil is on the sheet.

7 Continue the seaweed to give the illusion that it is behind the fish. Expel the green pulp right up to the edge of the fish, then, when you continue underneath, make sure that you line it up with the strand of seaweed on top of the fish, as above.

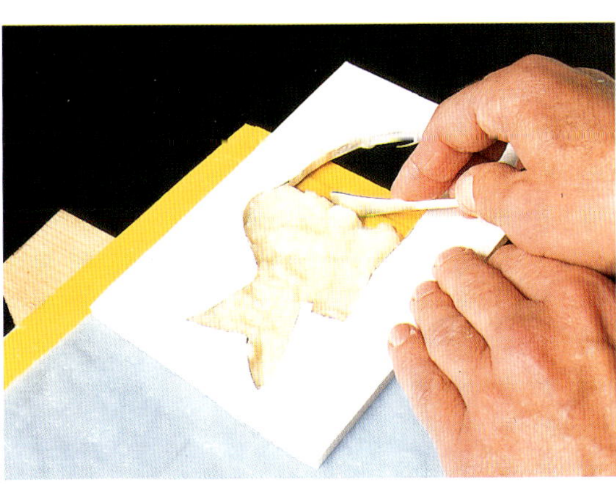

5 Apply the dilute yellow pulp as before and pack it down with the end of the spoon. Also use the end of the spoon to tidy up the edge of the half fish so that it lines up with the edge of the blue sheet.

8 Couch and press this sheet in the normal way and leave to dry on a melamine sheet.

dry papers

You can create stunning decorative effects with dry paper. Techniques such as spraying or paste papers are fairly simple to master, while making a linocut or weaving paper will take a little longer. Dry paper techniques can be practiced with bought handmade paper, but for a truly satisfying result, try them with paper you have created yourself.

Dry paper techniques

The techniques featured in this section are not an intrinsic part of the papermaking process, but are applied after the paper has been made. They can successfully be used on paper that you have made yourself, or on the variety of hand- or machine-made papers you can buy. Whatever paper you choose to use, you will find that with the minimum of practice you will soon be able to achieve some stunning finishes. On the face of it, some of these techniques seem simple, perhaps too simple. Yet this is the remarkable thing about them: it is

ABOVE *An abstract pattern or a realistic scene can be produced with stencil and spray on paper.*

Stencil and spray

YOU WILL NEED

- **Thin card**
- **Scissors**
- **11½ x 16½ in (A3) sheet of cartridge paper**
- **Spray diffuser**
- **Ink, yellow, green, and red**
- **Craft knife**

2 Spray over the shapes once again, this time with green ink, moving across the paper steadily from left to right to achieve an even spread of spray. Remove and reposition the shapes and spray with the red ink.

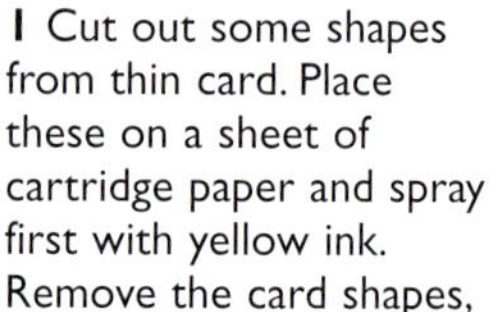

1 Cut out some shapes from thin card. Place these on a sheet of cartridge paper and spray first with yellow ink. Remove the card shapes, using a craft knife to lift them up to avoid smudging the wet ink. Reposition the shapes in new positions on the sheet of paper.

3 Use a craft knife to lift the shapes for the last time to reveal a uniquely patterned sheet of paper.

because of their ease of operation that you are able, with a little practice, to gain unique effects. Although they produce fantastic results spraying and splattering techniques are very messy. As there is a danger of covering areas beyond your sheet of paper, make sure that the surrounding area is adequately protected with newspapers or a polythene sheet. There is no such problem when using a wax resist technique, where the wax is used in a similar way to a stencil by masking out areas of the paper during the application of paint.

ABOVE *Cartridge paper sprayed with acrylic inks has been torn into strips, folded, and woven in different directions.*

Splattering

YOU WILL NEED

- **Paintbrush**
- **Artist's acrylic paint, orange, blue, and black**
- **Small block of wood**
- **11½ x 16½ in (A3) sheet of sugar paper**
- **Old toothbrush**

1 Load a paintbrush with orange acrylic paint. Hold a small block of wood 2 in (5cm) above and parallel to the surface of a sheet of sugar paper and gently tap the side of the brush on the wood while, at the same time, moving across the sheet. Repeat with blue paint.

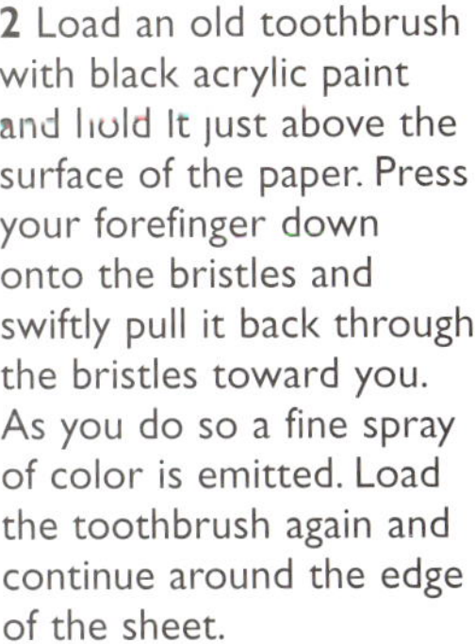

2 Load an old toothbrush with black acrylic paint and hold it just above the surface of the paper. Press your forefinger down onto the bristles and swiftly pull it back through the bristles toward you. As you do so a fine spray of color is emitted. Load the toothbrush again and continue around the edge of the sheet.

Wax resist

YOU WILL NEED

- **11½ x 16½ in (A3) sheet of cartridge paper**
- **Patterned, textured surface such as an iron grate**
- **Wax candle**
- **Cold water fabric dye, blue**
- **Plastic bowl**
- **Paintbrush**

1 Lay a sheet of cartridge paper over a patterned, textured surface, in this case an iron grate. Rub over the entire surface of the paper with the long edge of the candle.

2 Mix blue fabric dye with water following the manufacturer's instructions. Use a paintbrush to paint the sheet of paper with the dye. As you do so, the pattern of the iron grate is revealed where the wax resists the dye.

LEFT Dyes and wax were used to create this image on tissue paper and brown wrapping paper.

Batik is a traditional textile technique where wax is used to mask out areas of the fabric that will not be colored during the dyeing process. Here I have adapted the technique for use on a sheet of paper. The wax used has been melted and is applied hot by brush; in this instance I am using a pattern created by the brush itself. But with a little practice it is possible to obtain a more defined image.

Batik

YOU WILL NEED

- Wax pellets
- Wax melting pan or bain-marie
- Small paintbrush
- 11½ x 16½ in (A3) sheet of cartridge paper
- Cold water fabric dyes, yellow and green
- 2 plastic bowls
- Household paintbrush
- Newspaper, or newsprint paper (available from art shops)
- Iron
- Tjanting tool

1 Melt the wax pellets in a wax melting pan or bain-marie, following the manufacturer's instructions. Load a small paintbrush with molten wax and quickly brush it onto a sheet of cartridge paper to create a simple repeat design.

2 Mix yellow and green fabric dyes with water in separate bowls, following the manufacturer's instructions. Once the wax on the paper has hardened, use a household paintbrush to paint yellow fabric dye over the whole sheet. Rinse the brush.

LEFT The wax prevents the paint being absorbed into the paper and creates interesting effects.

Definition of the design or image can be further enhanced by the use of a Tjanting tool (a specialized tool for applying wax, available from craft stores), which I use here to produce a mass of spots over the paper. With practice you will be able to use this tool to draw a linear pattern or image.

RIGHT *Stunning colors and effects have been created with tissue paper, Chinese paper, dyes, and wax.*

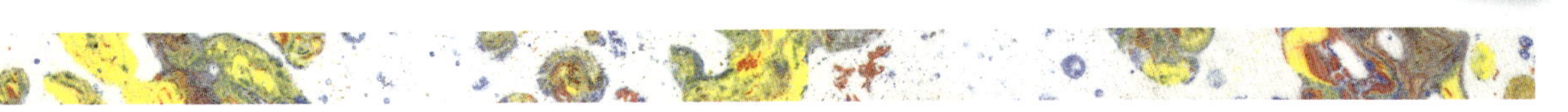

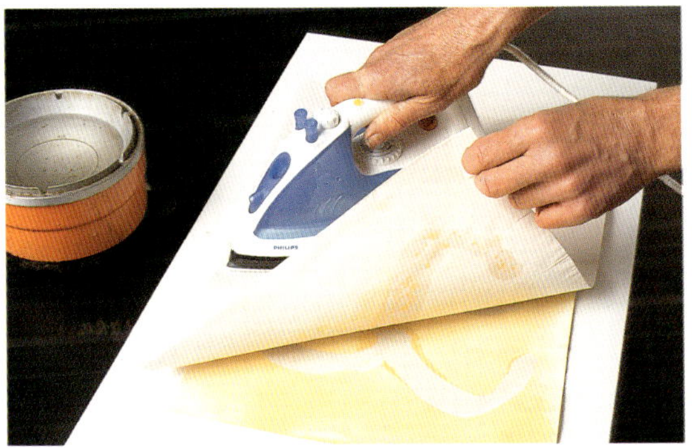

3 The paper will have soaked up some of the wax, but to remove the excess, lay a sheet of newspaper or newsprint paper on the waxed sheet and iron over it: this melts the wax which is in turn then absorbed by the newspaper.

5 When the wax spots have hardened, paint the surface of the paper with green fabric dye.

4 Before applying the second color, load a Tjanting tool with molten wax and let wax drop from it onto the paper to create a spotty effect.

6 Use the same sheet of newspaper to iron off the excess wax from the sheet. When you pull back the newspaper, an interesting batik paper will be revealed.

With the paste paper technique you can produce some stunning effects, and the thicker the layer of paint and paste mixture, the more three dimensional the finished effect will be. Try other items to draw the pattern, such as the end of a paintbrush, a sponge, a crumpled-up rag; in fact the list is endless. Do not feel constrained to making only patterned paste papers: also write or draw into the paste surface to achieve different effects.

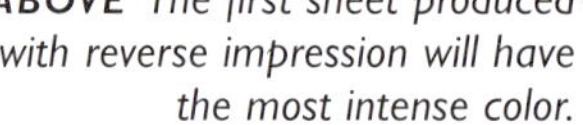

ABOVE *The first sheet produced with reverse impression will have the most intense color.*

Paste paper

YOU WILL NEED

- **Thin card**
- **Scissors**
- **2½ in (6.5cm) bulldog clip**
- **Wallpaper paste**
- **Plastic bowl**
- **Artist's acrylic paint, purple**
- **Spoon**
- **Paintbrush**
- **11½ x 16½ in (A3) sheet of cartridge paper**

BELOW *Whatever tool is used for the paste paper technique, a richly textured effect is achieved.*

1 Cut four small rectangles of card. Position the card pieces equally spaced apart in a large bulldog clip. Following the manufacturer's instructions, mix up a small amount of wallpaper paste in a bowl. Dilute paint to the consistency of single cream. Add to the paste and stir well to achieve the consistency of cottage cheese.

2 Generously load a paintbrush with the paint and paste mixture. Apply to a sheet of cartridge paper in broad strokes to obtain a thick and even layer over the whole surface.

3 Hold the bulldog clip paintbrush over the still-wet paint and use one continuous movement to pull it through the paint across the length of the paper, moving from left to right to create a wave pattern. Remove a piece of card from the clip and repeat the wavy movement next to the first impression.

4 Remove another piece of card from the clip and repeat the wave pattern. Finish by making a wave pattern with just one piece of card in the clip.

Initially using the same method to produce paste papers, reverse impression allows you to obtain more than one sheet of decorated paper from the same pattern, providing a good introduction to the concept of printing. Importantly the pattern on the paper will be a reverse of that drawn onto the board—bear this in mind if you decide to write or draw a specific image. The number of sheets you are able to obtain will depend on the thickness of the paste and paint mixture applied to the board, as will the intensity of color on each successive sheet.

ABOVE *Bought paper has been colored with raw pigments, then cut and glued together in strips of squares and triangles.*

Reverse impression

YOU WILL NEED

- **Wallpaper paste**
- **Plastic bowl**
- **Acrylic paint, purple**
- **Spoon**
- **Paintbrush**
- **Melamine sheet**
- **Cotton swab**
- **2 11½ x 16½ in (A3) sheets of cartridge paper**
- **Length of wood**

1 Make a wallpaper paste and paint mix following step 1 of Paste Paper (see page 100). Brush a thick layer of the paint and paste mix onto a melamine sheet, covering an area slightly larger than your sheet of paper.

2 Use a cotton swab to draw into the paint and paste mix on the melamine to create an interesting design, exploring a wide variety of marks.

3 Place a sheet of cartridge paper on top of the design and press down using a length of wood to apply an even but firm pressure over the whole surface of the paper.

4 Hold one corner of the paper and carefully peel back the sheet to reveal a print on the paper. Lie the sheet face up on a flat surface and allow to dry.

5 While there is still some paint and paste mix on the board, lay down another sheet of paper to create a second reverse impression. Apply firm and even pressure across the whole surface with the length of wood, and peel back the paper to reveal another, less intense print of the pattern.

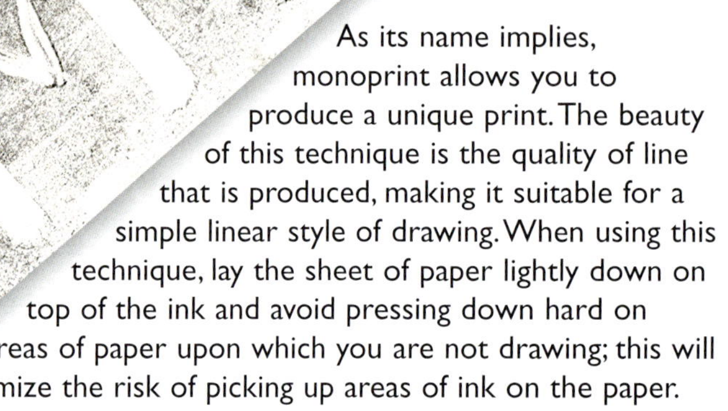

As its name implies, monoprint allows you to produce a unique print. The beauty of this technique is the quality of line that is produced, making it suitable for a simple linear style of drawing. When using this technique, lay the sheet of paper lightly down on top of the ink and avoid pressing down hard on areas of paper upon which you are not drawing; this will minimize the risk of picking up areas of ink on the paper.

LEFT *Monoprinting lends itself to a linear style of drawing. The lines contrast with the mottled effect of the ink residue that is left on the paper.*

Monoprint

YOU WILL NEED

- **Printing ink, black**
- **Melamine sheet**
- **Roller**
- **11½ x 16½ in (A3) sheet of cartridge paper**
- **Paintbrush**

1 Squeeze black printing ink from the tube onto a melamine sheet. Roll out the ink so that it covers an area slightly larger than your sheet of paper.

2 Lay a sheet of cartridge paper on the ink and with the end of a paintbrush draw a simple picture on the back. In this case I have drawn a hilly landscape within a frame.

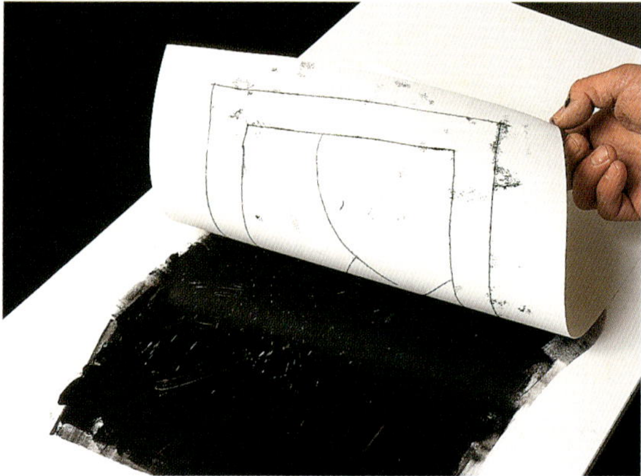

3 Carefully lift up one corner of the paper and slowly peel it back off the ink to reveal the pattern printed on the paper. Lay the sheet, face up, on a flat surface to dry.

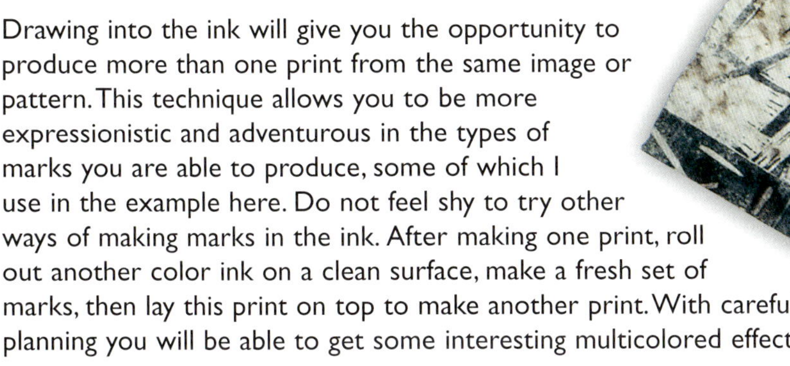

RIGHT *A variety of techniques were used to create this piece, including linocut and collage with embedded papers.*

Drawing into the ink will give you the opportunity to produce more than one print from the same image or pattern. This technique allows you to be more expressionistic and adventurous in the types of marks you are able to produce, some of which I use in the example here. Do not feel shy to try other ways of making marks in the ink. After making one print, roll out another color ink on a clean surface, make a fresh set of marks, then lay this print on top to make another print. With careful planning you will be able to get some interesting multicolored effects.

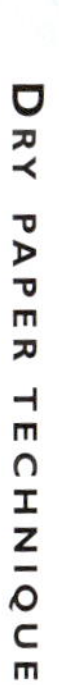

Drawing in ink

YOU WILL NEED

- **Printing ink, black**
- **Melamine sheet**
- **Roller**
- **Paintbrush**
- **Cotton swab**
- **Dishcloth**
- **11½ x 16½ in (A3) sheet of cartridge paper**

2 Lay a sheet of cartridge paper on top of the ink and brush over the entire back of the sheet with a firm and even pressure. Try not to let the paper move during the process. If you do, the pattern will smudge.

1 Follow step 1 of Monoprint (see page 102) to cover a melamine surface with black ink. Create a variety of marks in the ink using a variety of implements. Here I have used the end of a paintbrush, a cotton swab, and a dishcloth.

3 Gently lift up a corner of the sheet and peel it away from the board. A print of the design that was first made on the board will now be revealed on the paper. Leave the print to dry face up on a flat surface.

ABOVE A printing grid was used with this linocut in order to get the pattern to match up perfectly each time.

A linocut is an efficient and economical way to make a printing block that is suitable for printing by hand without the need for any specialist equipment. By producing a simple design I show you how it is possible to repeat this pattern to create a coherent overall patterning effect using two colors. When designing the pattern the main consideration to bear in mind will be its ability to repeat itself. It helps when designing the pattern to go for a symmetrical design, as this will ensure that when placed side by side,

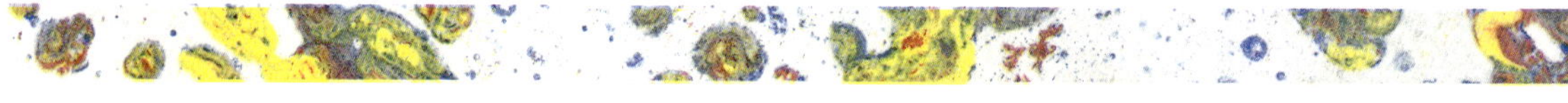

Linocut

YOU WILL NEED

- **4 x 3 in (10 x 7.5cm) piece of linoleum**
- **Pencil**
- **Pair of compasses**
- **Ruler**
- **Linoleum cutting tool with narrow and broad blades**
- **Cutting mat**
- **11½ x 16½ in (A3) sheet of copy paper**
- **Masking tape**
- **8 x 12 in (20 x 30cm) sheet of cotton linters paper (see pages 22–23 and 28–41)**
- **Printing ink, black and red**
- **2 sheets of glass**
- **Roller**
- **Spoon**

1 Draw a 2 in (5cm) diameter circle in the center of a piece of linoleum. Draw a ¼ in (6mm) wide band through the center of the circle. Draw another ¼ in (6mm) wide band across the linoleum at right angles to the first.

2 Using a narrow blade in a linoleum cutting tool and working over a cutting mat, carefully gouge along the drawn lines. Remember always to keep both hands behind the cutting blade.

3 Fix a broad blade into the cutting tool and cut away the linoleum on the outside of the motif between the lines, working away from the design toward the outer edges to prevent the design getting accidentally damaged.

4 Finally, carefully cut out the central square of the design.

5 To ensure that the final printed design joins up, make a printing grid that corresponds to the size of the paper you are printing onto. Tape a sheet of copy paper to your work surface and draw a line vertically down the center. Draw five parallel lines horizontally across the sheet, each 3 in (7.5cm) apart so as to correspond with the width of the linoleum tile.

6 Mark the center point of the top edge of a sheet of handmade cotton linters paper. Line this up with the top horizontal and center line of the printing grid. Tape the top edge of the handmade paper in this position.

the extremities of the design join up so giving a cohesive surface across the paper. Another way to achieve a similar effect of an overall pattern is to ink up the linocut and print directly onto the sheet of paper. The drawback when using this method is that it will be more difficult to match up the printed design each time.

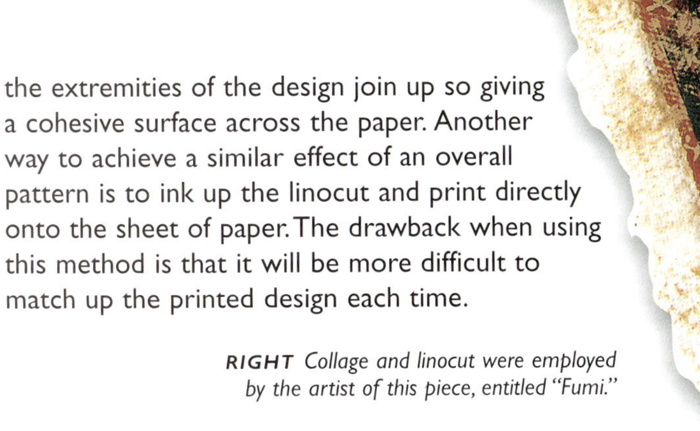

RIGHT *Collage and linocut were employed by the artist of this piece, entitled "Fumi."*

7 Use a roller to apply black printing ink to the linocut. To ink up the linocut, squeeze some printing ink onto a sheet of glass. Roll the ink out over the surface of the glass to produce an even layer on the roller. Roll the inked roller over the raised areas of the linocut. Wash the roller in water after use and use a separate sheet of glass to roll out the red ink used in step 10.

9 Fold back the handmade paper to reveal the print. Repeat, positioning the linocut in alternate squares on the grid.

8 Position the black inked linocut on one of the squares in the printing grid. Fold the handmade paper over the top of the inked-up linocut. Rub the paper with the back of a spoon, applying a firm and even pressure. Reapply ink after each print.

10 Repeat the printing process using red ink and positioning the linocut in the opposite alternate grid positions.

The purpose of the printing grid now becomes clear: it allows the repeated design to line up accurately.

Classic marbling involves the creation of a complex repeated pattern on the surface of water, which is then transferred onto a sheet of paper. It is a technique that requires a great deal of skill and practice and it is fair to say that marbling in its proper sense is not for the faint hearted. However, using the simplified technique I describe here, you will be able not only to grasp the basic principles of this ancient craft but also to produce some stunning colored papers. This method of marbling, as well as being quick, affords

LEFT AND RIGHT *Fantastic colors and effects are produced by this simple marbling technique. The oil paints float and disperse on the surface of the water producing unique patterns every time.*

Marbling

YOU WILL NEED

- **Oil paints, yellow, blue, and red**
- **Mineral spirits**
- **4 plastic bowls**
- **Eye dropper**
- **Shallow tray**
- **Paintbrush**
- **8 x 12 in (20 x 30cm) sheet of cotton linters paper (see pages 22–23 and 28–41)**
- **Newspaper**

1 Mix each of the three oil colors with mineral spirits in a separate bowl and part fill a fourth bowl with water. To check the consistency of each oil paint mix, take up a small amount in an eye dropper and add a drop to the surface of the water.
If the paint stays on top of the water and slowly starts to disperse outward, as shown above, then you have the correct consistency. If the paint disperses immediately you will need to add more paint, and, conversely, if it does not disperse you will need to add more mineral spirits.

2 Half fill a shallow tray with water and add drops of each color to the surface of the water. Spread the colors randomly across the surface.

3 Dip the end of a paintbrush into the water and move it through in a haphazard fashion to create an interesting swirling effect.

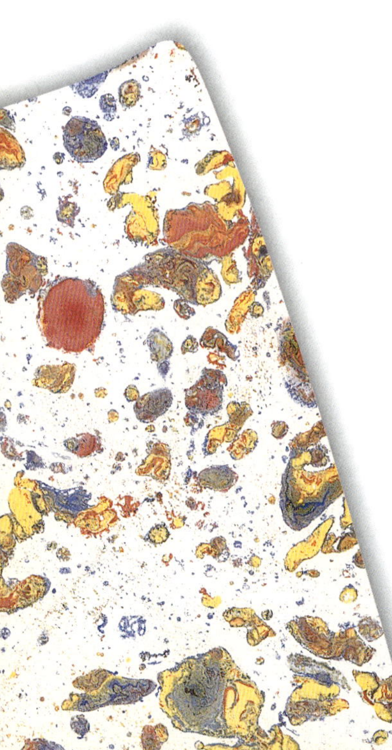

LEFT *Use tiny drops of oil colors and do not swirl the water to achieve this effect.*

you the opportunity to produce any number of uniquely patterned papers. Although I advise using oil paints because they will float on the surface of the water longer, it is also possible to get similar effects with acrylic paints, colored inks, or specialized marbling colors that are available from art and craft shops.

4 Hold a sheet of cotton linters paper by diagonally opposite corners. Lower the sheet into the water, letting the center of the sheet touch the water first before lowering the edges down.

5 Let the sheet float on top of the water for a few seconds, then take hold of a corner and carefully lift it away from the surface. Lay the sheet paint-side up on newspaper to dry. You may find that there is enough paint left on the surface of the water in the tray to make another marbled paper, with a different pattern.

6 Before adding more paint to create a fresh marbled sheet, clean the surface of the water. Fold a newspaper into a 3 in (7.5cm) wide strip that is as long as the width of the tray. Hold it at a slight diagonal at the far end of the tray. Ensure the bottom edge is just touching the surface of the water as you slowly drag it across the surface toward you. The paint residue will be dragged along too. Tilt the newspaper up to scoop up the paints.

The roots of the folding and dyeing techniques shown below lie in their use in textile design. Because of this I am using a strong Japanese tissue paper, which is suitable for scrunching, folding, and then returning to its original shape in a similar way to fabric. Although I have used fabric dyes in these techniques, similar effects can be obtained using inks or acrylic colors. The scrunch and dye technique allows you to produce a random-colored pattern over the whole surface of the paper that is different each time.

LEFT AND BELOW Softly blended colors are easily produced with scrunch and dye techniques.

Scrunch and dye

YOU WILL NEED

- **Cold water fabric dyes, yellow, red, and blue**
- **3 plastic bowls**
- **9 x 12 in (23 x 30cm) sheet of Japanese tissue paper**
- **Protective gloves**
- **Dishcloth**

1 Carefully following the manufacturer's instructions, mix three fabric dyes with water, in three separate bowls.

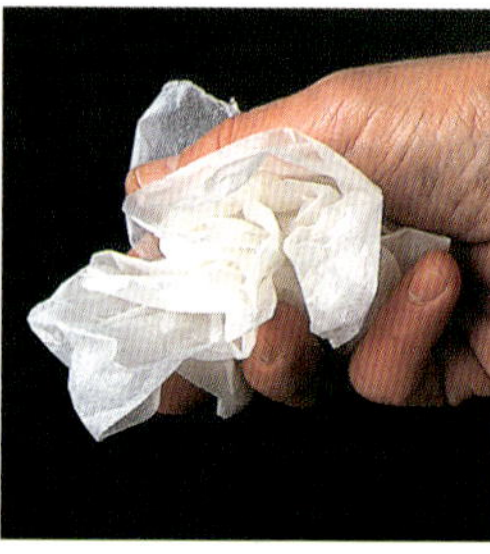

2 Take a sheet of tissue paper and scrunch it up between your fingers or in the palm of your hand.

3 Wearing protective gloves, dip the scrunched paper into the yellow dye. Do not dip it in too far because the paper is very absorbent and you do not want the whole sheet to absorb this one color.

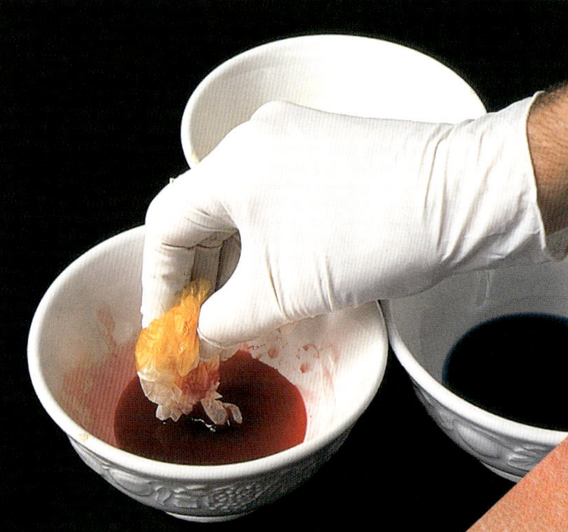

4 Turn the scrunched paper over in the hand to reveal an undyed area of tissue. Dip this portion of paper into the red dye.

RIGHT *This collage includes brown wrapping paper that has been dyed and hand stitched.*

Fold and dye techniques will allow you much more control over the final patterning effect than scrunch and dye. Whether it be the size of, or the number of folds, there are no hard and fast rules governing the way the paper is folded, although you will find it easier if you use a square piece of paper—the principle being that if you use a repetitive method to fold the paper you will achieve a regular repetitive pattern, whether that be a series of concentric circles or a regular grid pattern.

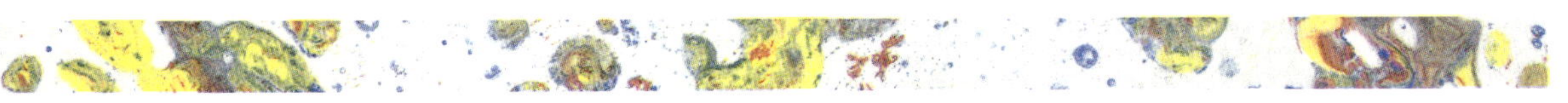

Fold and dye

YOU WILL NEED

- **Cold water fabric dyes, yellow, blue, and red**
- **3 plastic bowls**
- **10 in (25cm) square sheet of Japanese tissue paper**
- **Protective gloves**
- **Dishcloth**

1 Mix three fabric dyes with water, following the manufacturer's instructions, in three separate bowls.

2 Fold a sheet of Japanese tissue paper diagonally from corner to corner. Repeat twice more to create a triangular shape.

3 Wearing protective gloves, dip one corner of the paper triangle into the yellow dye.

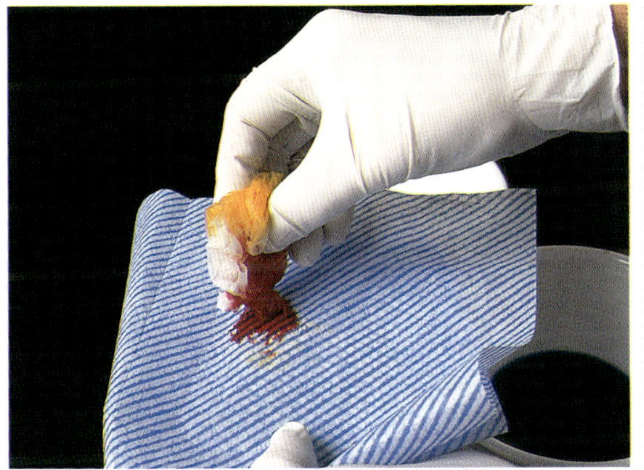

5 If the tissue paper absorbs too much dye, dab it on a dishcloth which will absorb the excess. Turn the bundle around to reveal the remaining undyed part. Dip this into the blue dye.

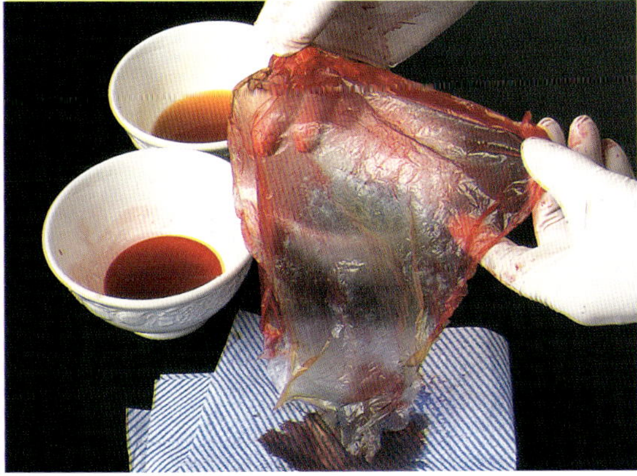

6 Carefully unfold the tissue to reveal the color absorption, and lay it on a smooth surface to dry.

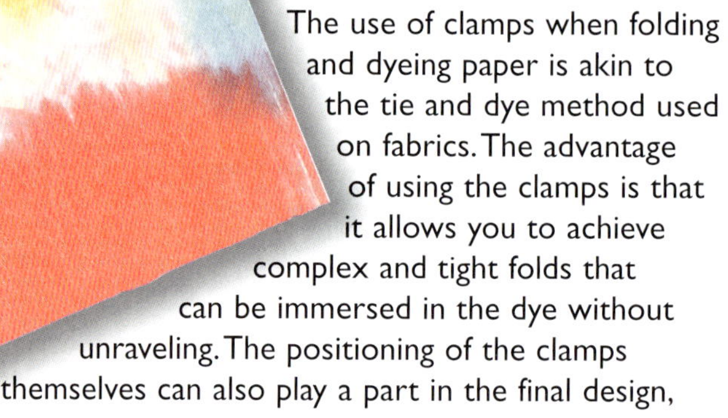

The use of clamps when folding and dyeing paper is akin to the tie and dye method used on fabrics. The advantage of using the clamps is that it allows you to achieve complex and tight folds that can be immersed in the dye without unraveling. The positioning of the clamps themselves can also play a part in the final design,

LEFT *The fold and dye technique provides some control over the pattern that can be achieved.*

4 Turn the triangle around and dip another corner into the blue dye.

5 To stop the dye being absorbed by the whole tissue sheet, dab the dyed corner into a dishcloth that will absorb any excess.

6 Turn the triangle around and dip the final corner into the red dye.

7 Use the dishcloth to absorb excess dye, and open out the tissue paper to reveal the design. Lay the tissue on a smooth surface to dry.

because by masking off areas of the paper they prevent impregnation by the dye. Finally, it is possible to use other types of paper with these folding techniques. As long as the paper isn't too thick, so that it can be easily folded, you will be able to produce interesting patterns and color variations.

ABOVE *"Two Studies," created with tissue paper on Nepalese paper and using dyes and wax.*

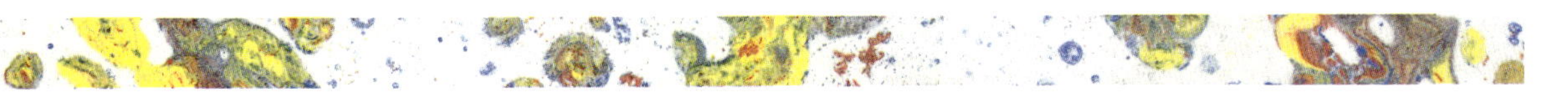

Fold and dye with clamps

YOU WILL NEED

- **Cold water fabric dyes, yellow and red**
- **2 plastic bowls**
- **9 x 12 in (23 x 30cm) sheet of Japanese tissue paper**
- **2 1¼ in (3cm) bulldog clips**
- **Protective gloves**
- **Dishcloth**

1 Mix two fabric dyes with water, following the manufacturer's instructions, in separate bowls.

2 Fold a sheet of tissue paper accordian-style along its length to produce a 1½ in (4cm) wide strip. Roll the strip tightly along its length and hold it in place with a bulldog clip.

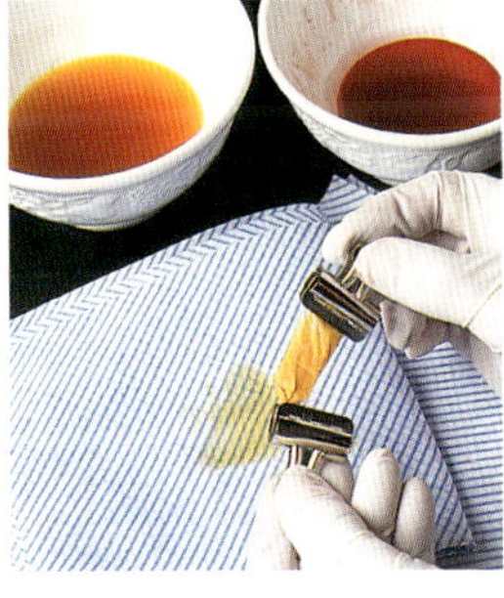

3 Wearing protective gloves, hold the roll by the clip and dip it into the yellow dye. Dab the dyed paper into a dishcloth to remove excess dye. Use a second bulldog clip to hold the dyed end of the tissue while you release the first clip.

4 Hold the paper by the new clip and dip it into the red dye, being careful not to go down too far into the dye.

5 Use the dishcloth to remove excess dye.

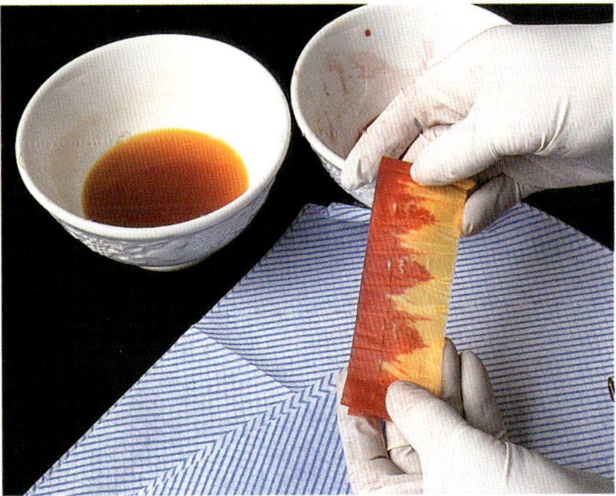

6 Carefully unravel the tissue paper to reveal the repeated pattern and lay it flat on a smooth surface to dry.

An embossed sheet of paper has a raised area either in the form of a design or typescript. This effect can be achieved mechanically with a printing press or more satisfactorily by hand as shown in the technique below. Using a stencil, an area of the sheet of paper is pushed into the stencil with an embossing tool. The paper you use needs to be thick as there is a chance that it can tear if it is too thin. Although you will be able to buy specialist embossing stencils, there are suitable alternatives such

ABOVE *Embossing stencils can be bought, or you can make a personal stencil of your own.*

Embossing

YOU WILL NEED

- **Masking tape**
- **Double-sided adhesive tape**
- **Embossing stencil**
- **6 x 8 in (15 x 20cm) sheet of Heritage paper, or any thick, heavyweight cartridge paper**
- **Embossing tool**

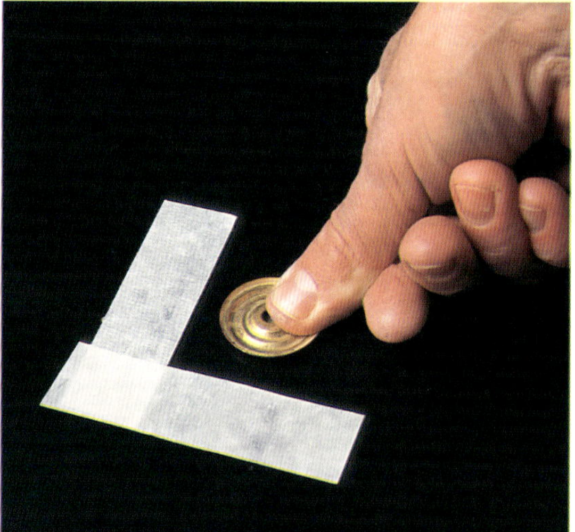

1 To make a registration mark, stick two 3 in (7.5cm) lengths of masking tape to your work surface to make a right angle. Use double-sided adhesive tape to fix an embossing stencil centrally within this angle. Press the stencil firmly into position.

2 Position the corner of a sheet of Heritage paper on the stencil and line it up with the registration marks. Use masking tape to fix the paper in position. Run your finger around the inside of the stencil to create the first impression on the paper.

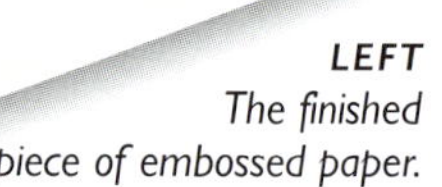

LEFT *The finished piece of embossed paper.*

as plastic drawing or lettering stencils, or found objects as in the example below, where I am using the brass backplate of a door handle. The main proviso when selecting a suitable stencil is that it has a well-defined edge or profile containing a recessed area. It is into this area that the paper is slowly and methodically pushed with the embossing tool. By rubbing the paper with even, consistent strokes, the paper is softened and pushed into the stencil, hard up against the interior surface.

ABOVE *"Sea Cell," formed from recycled paper and manipulated by hand.*

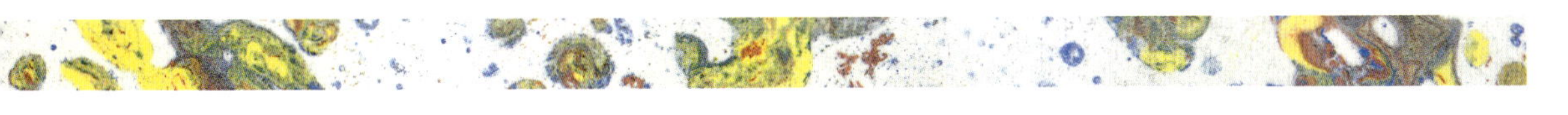

3 Carefully push an embossing tool around the inside edge of the stencil. By gradually increasing the amount of pressure you impart you will be able to push the paper into the stencil. As the paper starts to soften, begin venturing toward the center of the stencil, working diagonally back and forth.

4 As you increase the rubbing pressure the paper will be pushed further into the stencil. Continue until you have a satisfactory impression of the stencil.

5 Release the tape holding the paper in place and reposition another corner within the registration marks to ensure that the embossed pattern is in the same position on each corner of the sheet. Repeat steps 3–5 to emboss each corner.

6 Turn the sheet over to reveal the raised impression left on the right side of the paper.

A technique formulated by artists at the beginning of the 20th century, collage continues to be part of the artist's repertoire. For many of us, collage is likely to conjure up memories of school days! Do not let this cloud your judgment, because collage is an incredibly creative and adaptable technique. In the collage I make in the technique below, I have deliberately shied away from using scissors or a knife to cut the paper, preferring instead to introduce three different methods of tearing the paper. The resultant torn edge provides an interesting and effective contrast

ABOVE *Let your imagination run wild. Texture, shape, and color combine to make an interesting collage.*

Collage

YOU WILL NEED

- **14½ x 19 in (37 x 48.5cm) sheets of Indian handmade paper, yellow, pink, red, and blue**
- **Plate**
- **Steel ruler**
- **2 paintbrushes**
- **Craft glue (PVA)**
- **Roller**

1 Use a yellow sheet of Indian handmade paper as the base sheet. Lay a pink sheet directly on top. Hold a plate over the bottom left-hand corner of the sheet and tear the pink paper along the curved edge of the plate.

2 Remove the pink quarter circle and lay a red sheet along the bottom edge of the yellow sheet. Reposition the pink quadrant in the bottom left corner. Place a steel ruler on top of the sheets, lining it up with the bottom edge of the paper, and tear the red paper along the edge of the ruler.

3 Tear a freehand spiral from a blue sheet of handmade paper.

against the texture of the handmade Indian paper. Of course, the paper can be cut using scissors or a knife. The hard, clean edges produced would work well in a more geometric abstract design or an architectural cityscape. There are no restraints on the type of paper that can be used when making a collage, so spend some time in selecting the textures and colors of paper you will use.

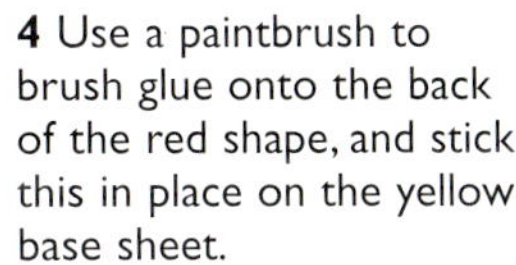

4 Use a paintbrush to brush glue onto the back of the red shape, and stick this in place on the yellow base sheet.

ABOVE *Decorated papers have been brought together to stunning effect in this collage entitled "Icon."*

5 Use a clean, dry paintbrush to brush the red shape into position, working from the middle out toward the edges to expel any trapped air.

6 Follow steps 4–5 to stick the pink and blue shapes on. Finally, work a roller over the whole collage to make sure all the pieces are stuck down.

For the paper sandwich technique to succeed it is essential that a thin paper is used to ensure that whatever is sandwiched is clearly visible. It is a technique that needs to be carried out with great care because it is very easy for the delicate tissue paper to tear—this is more likely to happen if you choose to sandwich bulky or sharp-edged items such as the pumpkin seeds I use on page 118. When selecting an object to embed, choose one that the top layer of tissue will easily wrap around. You could

Paper sandwich: with a feather

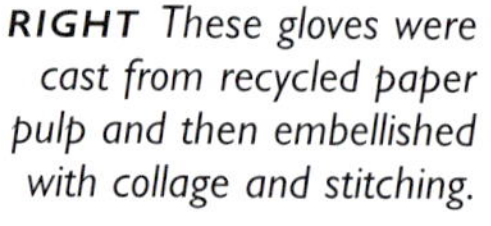

RIGHT *These gloves were cast from recycled paper pulp and then embellished with collage and stitching.*

YOU WILL NEED

- **2 9 x 12 in (23 x 30cm) sheets of Japanese tissue paper**
- **Polythene sheet to protect the work surface**
- **Peacock feather**
- **Fine paintbrush**
- **Paintbrush**
- **Craft glue (PVA)**
- **Sponge**

1 Lay a sheet of Japanese tissue paper on top of the polythene sheet. Position a peacock feather centrally on the paper and use a fine paintbrush to splay it out.

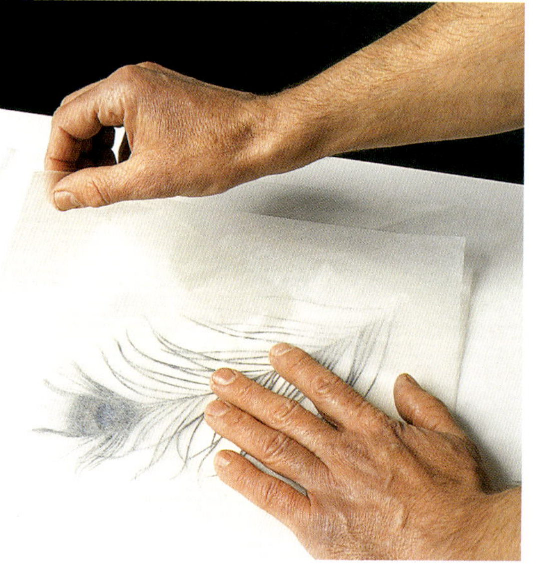

2 Carefully lay a second sheet of tissue paper directly on top of the first sheet and feather. Take great care not to disturb the feather.

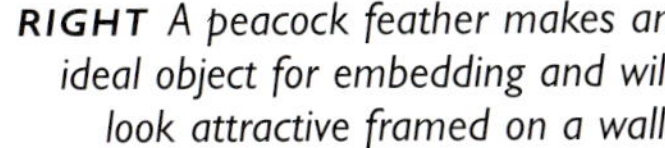

RIGHT A peacock feather makes an ideal object for embedding and will look attractive framed on a wall.

3 Load a paintbrush with glue and, starting from the center of the feather, which you can see through the top sheet of paper, brush the glue onto the paper, working along the center of the feather before going out toward the edges. Cover the entire surface with glue so that it soaks through the sheet underneath.

4 Working from the center out again, use a sponge to push out any trapped air between the two sheets, taking care not to rip the wet paper.

5 Leave the paper to dry overnight on the polythene. The two sheets have bonded to become one, with the feather in between, and can be easily lifted off the polythene to reveal a very shiny surface that mirrors the surface of the polythene.

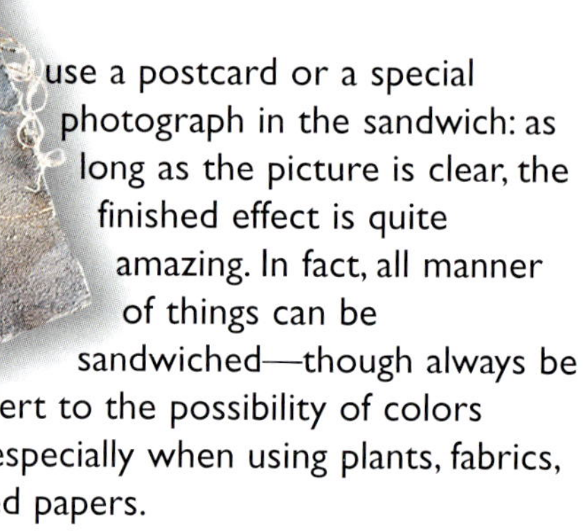

use a postcard or a special photograph in the sandwich: as long as the picture is clear, the finished effect is quite amazing. In fact, all manner of things can be sandwiched—though always be alert to the possibility of colors running, especially when using plants, fabrics, or colored papers.

LEFT *Fabric dyes and acrylic paints were applied to wet newsprint paper. Thread was stitched on and more color was added.*

Paper sandwich: with petals and seeds

YOU WILL NEED

- **2 9 x 11 in (23 x 28cm) sheets of mulberry paper (available from craft stores)**
- **12 in (30cm) square polythene sheet**
- **Pumpkin seeds**
- **Petals**
- **Paintbrush**
- **Craft glue (PVA)**
- **Craft knife**

1 Lay a sheet of mulberry paper on a polythene sheet and then position pumpkin seeds around the edge of the paper. Arrange the petals in the center of the sheet.

2 Lay a second sheet of mulberry paper directly on top of the first sheet and the seeds and petals, taking care not to dislodge the arrangement.

LEFT *The artist created this embedded piece by pouring pulp onto string laid in the frame.*

LEFT *Embedding raised objects such as seeds can be difficult because the delicate paper is easily torn.*

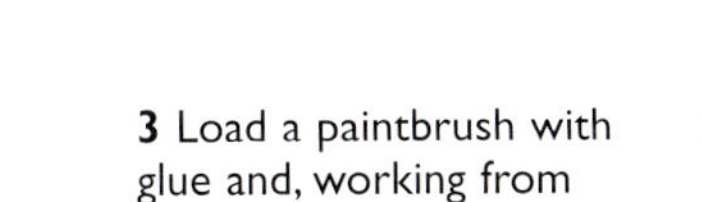

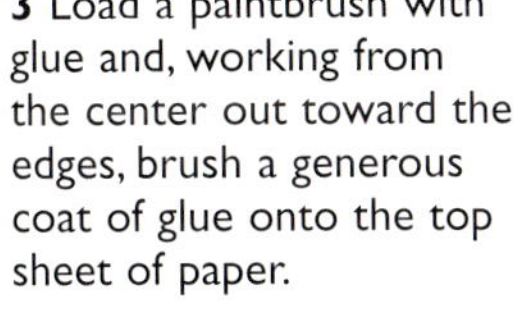

3 Load a paintbrush with glue and, working from the center out toward the edges, brush a generous coat of glue onto the top sheet of paper.

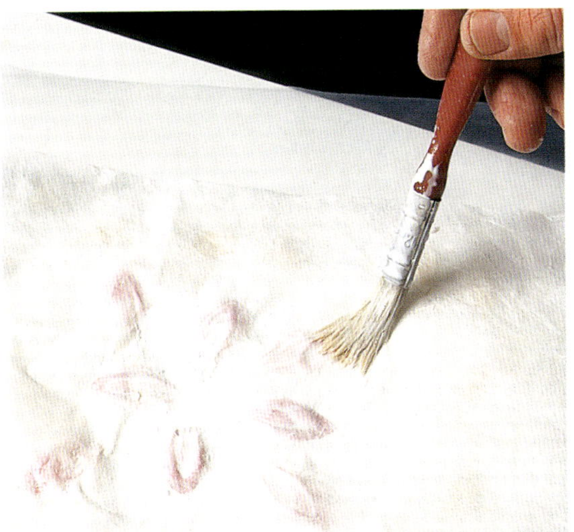

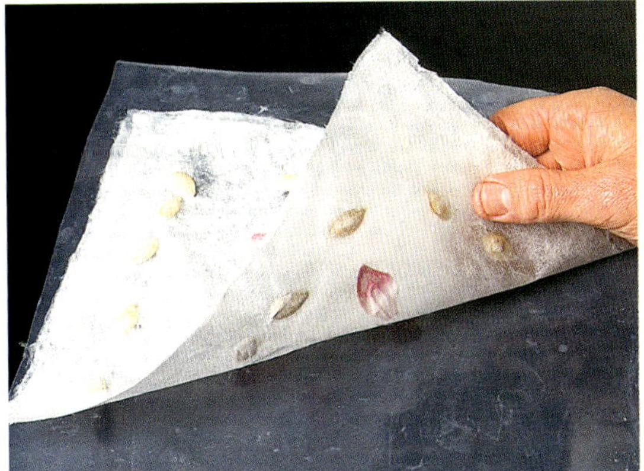

4 With bulky inclusions it is necessary to pierce the top layer of paper to expel air and to ensure that it lies flat. Do this by carefully cutting a slit by a bulky addition with a craft knife and immediately brushing it down flat onto the sheet below.

5 Leave the paper on the polythene sheet to dry overnight. The two sheets will bond to become one, with the seeds and petals in between, and can be lifted off the polythene to reveal a very shiny surface that mirrors the surface of the polythene.

LEFT *With an artist's eye and skill, woven paper becomes a work of art.*

Since paper was first made it has been woven, although in the early days the paper would have been twisted to produce the threads for the warp and weft of a loom. The warp threads are those that run lengthwise, while the weft threads run horizontally across, under and over each of the warp threads in turn. It is possible to achieve a variety of interesting effects by weaving together flat strips of paper. These strips can be made by tearing or by cutting with a knife, such as in the first technique here, where I have varied the width of both the warp and weft to create an

Weaving paper

YOU WILL NEED

- **9¾ x 13¾ in (24.5 x 35cm) sheet of white parchment paper**
- **Steel ruler**
- **Pencil**
- **Craft knife**
- **Cutting mat**
- **9¾ x 13¾ in (24.5 x 35cm) sheet of yellow parchment paper**
- **Masking tape**
- **Double-sided adhesive tape**

BELOW *Tissue paper is ideal for weaving because it comes in such glorious colors.*

1 To make the warp threads, that run lengthwise, make marks across a sheet of white parchment paper, starting ½ in (1.5cm) from the top edge. Mark out five ⅜ in (1cm) divisions, six at ¼ in (6mm), six at ½ in (1.5cm), six at ¼ in (6mm), and five at ⅜ in (1cm). Repeat these divisions along the bottom edge of the paper. Line the ruler up along the marks and cut the strips, using a craft knife over a cutting mat, right to the bottom of the sheet.

2 To make the weft strips, that run widthwise, mark the following divisions along both of the longer edges of a sheet of yellow parchment paper: 12 at ½ in (1.5cm), 12 at ⅜ in (1cm), and 12 at ¼ in (6mm). Use the steel ruler and craft knife over a cutting mat to cut the strips.

3 Tape the top of the warp strips to the work surface and weave three ½ in (1.5cm) weft strips in and out of the warp. Next, weave three ⅜ in (1cm) strips, then three ¼ in (6mm) strips. Continue weaving the weft in the same order.

undulating subtle color effect across the surface of the weaving. In the second technique, using torn strips, I have gone for a more rough and ready look, showing how it is possible to weave flimsy paper to increase its strength, and taking advantage of the availability of brightly colored tissue paper.

***RIGHT** Banana fiber pulp was used to create the paper, which was then torn into strips and woven.*

4 You will find that as you proceed you need to push up the weft strips with the craft knife to keep the weaving nice and tight.

5 As you reach the end of the weaving, fix the warp and weft ends together with double-sided adhesive tape to keep the whole woven sheet intact.

Torn paper weaving

YOU WILL NEED

- **Tissue paper, 3 24 x 30 in (60 x 75cm) sheets each of pink, green, yellow, blue, and red**
- **Steel ruler**
- **Craft knife**
- **Double-sided adhesive tape**

1 Fold each paper sheet in two to create 15 x 24 in (38 x 60cm) sheets. Using a steel ruler as a guide, tear off 1 in (2.5cm) wide strips.

2 Arrange the red strips on your work surface as the warp, and then weave alternate colors of tissue paper weft strips. Push up the weft strips with a craft knife where necessary to keep the weaving nice and tight. Once finished, secure the ends of the warp and weft strips with double-sided adhesive tape.

also see the following page
Dry techniques: paper sandwich: with a feather 116

Project 5

Bamboo scroll

This project has an oriental theme. Bamboo strips—bamboo was one of the earliest sources of fiber used to make paper—are sandwiched between sheets of Japanese tissue paper. The resulting paper looks particularly attractive hanging directly on the wall, or in front of a window to take full advantage of its translucency and the differing qualities of each side: one side is shiny and shows the inside of the bamboo, while the other side is matte and reveals the outside of the bamboo. It is absolutely essential that you use split bamboo, and you may be able to purchase bamboo that has already been split. However, if you do split it yourself, make sure it is held firmly in a vise or by clamps before you begin the operation.

YOU WILL NEED

- **3 7½ in (19cm) lengths of bamboo**
- **Vise or clamps**
- **Heavy duty craft knife**
- **Hammer**
- **2 12 x 18 in (30 x 45.5cm) sheets of Japanese tissue paper**
- **Large polythene sheet to protect the work surface**
- **Paintbrush**
- **Craft glue (PVA)**
- **Sponge**
- **Craft knife**
- **Double-sided adhesive tape**
- **2 13¼ in (33.5cm) lengths of bamboo**

1 Hold a length of bamboo vertically in a vise or clamps. Place the craft knife halfway across the top of the bamboo. Use a hammer to force the knife down into the bamboo to split it. After a while it will be possible to pull the stick apart in a clean break because the bamboo will split lengthwise along its grain. Repeat for the remaining two lengths of bamboo.

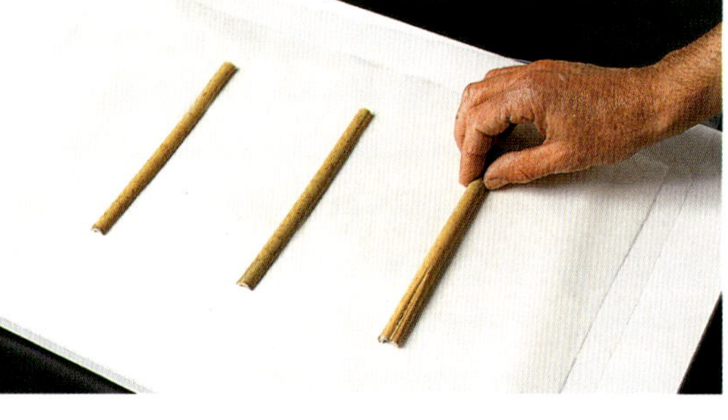

2 Lay a sheet of Japanese tissue paper on a polythene sheet and position three lengths of split bamboo equidistant and horizontal to one another.

3 Position a second sheet of Japanese tissue paper directly on top of the first, making sure that the edges of the two sheets line up all the way around.

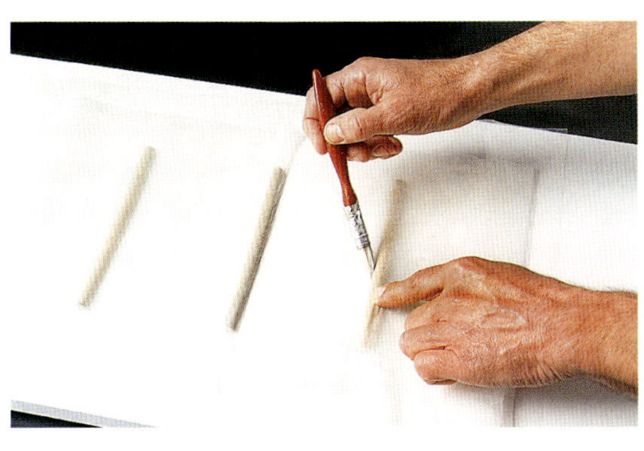

4 Load a paintbrush with glue and, starting at the middle length of bamboo, brush the glue onto the paper over the bamboo. Brush from the center outward, pushing the brush right up to the bamboo. Cover the entire surface. When brushing up to each of the bamboo lengths, hold the wood in position so that it does not become dislodged.

5 Starting at the center, sponge the paper out toward the sides to expel any air trapped between the two sheets. Use even, outward strokes parallel to the bamboo lengths.

6 At the end of each bamboo strip there will be a bubble of air that will need sealing. To do this, use a craft knife to carefully cut along the top of the raised area of tissue at the end of each bamboo length, as above.

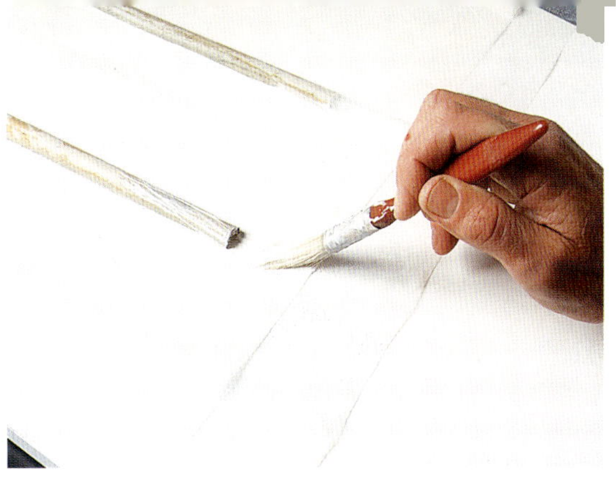

7 Paint down the cut areas with glue, then use the sponge to push the tissue down into place.

8 Leave the composite sheet to dry overnight on the polythene. The two sheets will have bonded to become one, with the bamboo in between, and are translucent. Gently lift back the sheet, taking care not to tear it.

9 Cut two lengths of double-sided adhesive tape to the width of the tissue paper, and stick each strip centrally onto a 13¼ in (33.5cm) length of whole bamboo. Peel away the backing paper and tape the bamboo to the tissue paper to make a wall hanging.

Suppliers list

UNITED STATES

Seastone Papers
Hand Papermaking and Book Arts
PO Box 331
West Tisbury
Martha's Vineyard, MA 02575
Phone: (508) 693 5786
Email: **sbernat@tiac.net**

Earth Pulp and Paper Products
PO Box 64
Legget, CA 95585
Email: **fulgin@aol.com**

Hiromi Paper International
2525 Michigan Ave, no.G9
Santa Monica, CA 90404
Phone: (310) 998 0098
Fax: (310) 998 0028

Botanical Paperworks
Phone: (204) 956 7393
Fax: (204) 956 5397
Email: **info@botanicalpaperworks.com**

Atlantic Earthworks
21 Winters Lane
Catonsville, MD 21228
Phone: 1 800 323 2811

Papershops.com
Phone: (805) 965 5574
Email: **paper@papershops.com**
Website: **www.papershops.com**

The Church of the Living Tree
PO Box 64
Leggett, CA 95585
Phone: (707) 925 6494
Fax: (707) 925 6472
Email: **tree@tree.org**
Website: **www.tree.org**

Crane & Co., Inc.
Continuum Papers
30 South St
Dalton, MA 01226
Phone: (800) 352 7789
Fax: (413) 499 3713
Email: **lagiusti@crane.com**
Website: **www.crane.com**

Twinrocker Hand Papermakers
100 East Third St
Brookston, IN 47923
Phone: (765) 563 3119

Pyramid Atlantic
6001 66th Ave
Suite 103
Riverdale, MD 20737
Phone: (301) 459 7154
Fax: (301) 577 8779

ArtPaper Inc.
Phone: (828) 296 0404
Email: **info@artpaper.com**
Website: **www.artpaper.com**

CANADA

The Papertrail
170 University Ave West
Suite 12-214
Waterloo, ON
N2L 3E9
Phone: (519) 884 7123
Fax: (519) 884 9655
Email: **info@papertrail.on.ca**

Arbokem
PO Box 95014
Vancouver, BC
V6P 6V4
Phone: (250) 613 9466
Website: **http://agripulp.com**

EcoSource Paper, Inc.
111–1841 Oak Bay Ave
Victoria, BC
V8R 3N6
Phone: 1 800 665 6944
Fax: (250) 370 1150
Email: **ecodette@island.net.com**
Website: **www.islandnet.com/~ecodette/ecosource.htm**

The Japanese Paper Place
887 Queen St. West
Toronto, ON
M6J 1G5
Phone: (416) 703 0089
Fax: (416) 703 0163
Email: **washi@japanesepaperplace.com**
Website:
www.japanesepaperplace.com

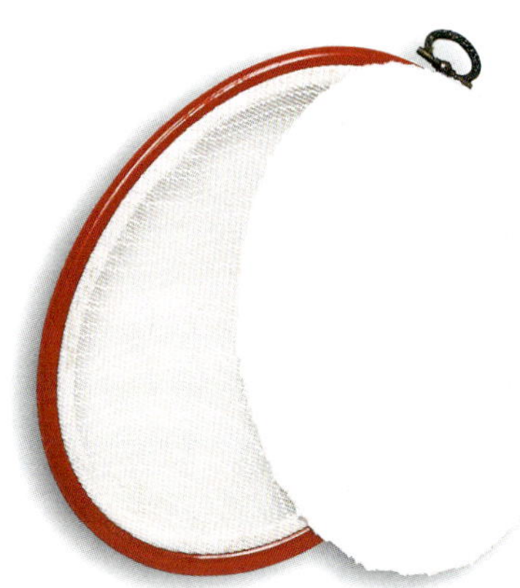

UNITED KINGDOM

Falkiner Fine Papers
76 Southampton Row
London WC1B 4AR
Phone (020) 7831 1151

Atlantis
7–9 Plumbers Row
London E1 1EQ
Phone (020) 7377 8855

Wookey Hole Papermill
Wookey Hole
Wells
Somerset
BA5 1BB
Phone: (0174) 967 2243
Email: **papermill@wookey.co.uk**

TreeFree
CHT Malthouse
Lyme Regis
Dorset
Phone: (0129) 744 3082

Phrazzle Card
29 Hest View Road
Ulverston
Cumbria
LA12 9PH
Phone/Fax: (01229) 588880
Email:
enquiries@phrazzlecard.co.uk
Website:
www.phrazzlecard.co.uk

Craftwork Cards
6 Park Gate Crescent
Guiseley
West Yorkshire
LS20 8AT
Phone/Fax: (01943) 878514
Email: **sue@craftworkcards.free serve.co.uk**
Website:
www.craftworkcards.f9.co.uk

Cranberry Card Co.
Phone: (01455) 551615
Fax: (01443) 224747
Email:
info@cranberrycards.co.uk
Website:
www.cranberrycards.co.uk

The Paper Shed
c/o Kath Russon
March House
Tollerton
York
YO6 2EQ
Phone: (01347) 838253
Fax: (01347) 838096
Email:
enquiries@papershed.com
Website: **www.papershed.com**

AUSTRALIA

Spicers Paper
82–90 Belmore Road
Riverwood
NSW
Phone: (02) 9534 5544

Papercrafts Mailbox
31 Garrett Street
Carrington
NSW 2294
Phone: (02) 4969 2543
Fax: (02) 4965 4726
Email: **ianola@coscom.net**
Web: **http://mailbox.safe shopper.com**

Paper House Express
339 Collier Road
Bassendean
WA 6054
Phone: (09) 240 1444

Paperpoint Sydney
21 Worth Street
Chullora
NSW 2190
Phone: (02) 9335 1460

Tomasetti Paper House
296 Ferntree Gully Road
Notting Hill
VIC 3168
Phone: (03) 8515 8880

Index

All techniques are illustrated. Page numbers in *italics* refer to illustrations of named works

Credits

Quarto would like to thank and acknowledge the following for supplying pictures reproduced in this book:

(Key: l left, r right, c center, t top, b bottom)

Barón, Maite: pp.2tl, 8b, 23, 47t, 51, 55, 95, 103, 105. **Tel**: +44 (0)20 8995 5812. Photographs by Euro Art.
Bullen, Stuart pp.18cl, 24, 25, 28b, 29, 37, 76c, 76-77b, 79, 80, 86. **Tel**: +44 (0)20 8838 5380. Photographs by Stuart Bullen.
Corner, Christa pp.5tr, 6tl, 6b, 9tl, 10b, 98, 99, 109, 111. **Tel**: +44 (0)1892 541 092. Photographs by James Corner.
Couzins-Scott, Elizabeth p.5c, 18br, 26, 67, 95, 115, 116. **Tel**: +44 (0)1253 890 867. Photographs by Peter Scott.
Farrow, Carol pp.2c, 7b, 8-9c, 10c, 18cr, 18bl, 19t, 30t, 31, 32, 44, 58-59, 60-61, 66. **Tel**: +44 (0)20 8461 0652. Photographs by Stephen Harper.
Gould, David pp.3, 18t, 20t, 22b, 36, 68, 69, 70. **Tel**: +44 (0)2920 255 088. Photographs by David Gould.
Harley-Peters, Janet pp.5tl, 94c, 101. **Tel**: +44 (0)20 7223 0274.
Hine, Henrietta pp. 9b, 11b, 27, 34, 72b. **Tel**: +44 (0)1273 564 346. Photographs by Henrietta Hine/Frimley Park NHS Hospital Trust.
Irsara, Irma pp.4b, 40, 41, 81. **Tel**: +44 (0)20 7272 2521. Website: www.oleary-irsara.com.
Kingsnorth, Jean pp.20-21b, 39, 43, 52, 77br, 88, 91. **Tel**: +44 (0)20 8360 7608. Photographs by Janine Rook.
Li, Han Fang, pp.2b, 11t, 21t, 78, 118t. **Tel**: +44 (0)161 279 0859. Photographs by Jill Green.
McGowan, Liz pp.7t, 38, 118b. **Tel**: +44 (0)1263 733 061.
Muhlert, Karin pp.4t, 9tr, 10tl, 11c, 113. **Tel**: +44 (0)1382 330 444. Photographs by Studio m, Malcolm Thomson.
Perrior, Janet pp.19b, 48, 97, 121. **Tel**: +44 (0)1929 481 149. Photographs by David Burnham.
Smith, Kate pp.2tr, 18c, 30b, 76b, 82, 84. **Tel**: +44 (0)1332 736 560.

All other papers by John Plowman.

While every effort has been made to credit contributors, Quarto would like to apologize should there have been any omissions or errors.